Also by Elizabeth Moran

Bradymania!

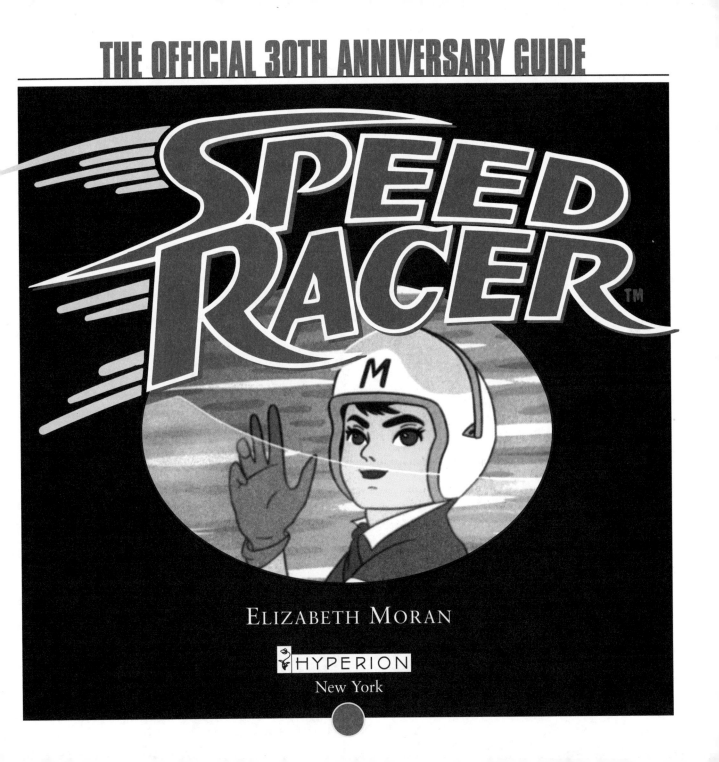

SPEED RACER™

ELIZABETH MORAN

HYPERION

New York

All *Speed Racer* artwork and related *Speed Racer* photos © 1997, Speed Racer Enterprises, Inc. *Speed Racer* is a trademark of Speed Racer Enterprises, Inc., and is used under license. All rights reserved.

Photos of Peter Fernandez and Jack Grimes, courtesy Michelle Talich.

Photo of Jack Curtis, courtesy Liane Curtis.

Photo of Corinne Orr, courtesy Corinne Orr.

Photos of Tatsuo Yoshida, Kenji Yoshida, and Ippei Kuri © 1967, Tatsunoko Production Co., Ltd.

Artwork of Tatsuo Yoshida's *Mach Go Go Go* manga, courtesy Tatsunoko Production Co., Ltd.

Photos of Speed turning the wheel, Tongue Blaggard, and Slash Marker, Jr., courtesy Personality Photos, Inc.

Photos of Bobby Labonte and his vehicle by Ernie Mache, Cameras in Action and Stock Photography. Reprinted by permission of James B. White and Bobby Labonte.

English translation of the Japanese theme song to *Mach Go Go Go* © 1967, Tatsunoko Production Co., Ltd. Reprinted by permission.

Photos of Volkswagen GTI and *Speed Racer* © 1996, Volkswagen. Reprinted by permission.

American version of *Speed Racer* theme song © Speed Racer Enterprises, Inc. All rights reserved.

NASCAR/ESPN commercial scripts © Speed Racer Enterprises, Inc. Used by permission of ESPN.

Mach 5 line art on pp. 15 and 17 illustrated by Tim Neil. Reprinted by permission.

Library of Congress Cataloging-in-Publication Data
Moran, Elizabeth.
    Speed racer : the official 30th anniversary guide /
Elizabeth Moran. — 1st ed.
      p.   cm.
    ISBN 0-7868-8246-8
    1. Speed racer (Television program)   I. Title.
PN1992.77.S6399M67   1997
791.45'72—dc21   97-3161
               CIP

FIRST EDITION
10 9 8 7 6 5 4 3 2 1

DESIGNED BY ROBERT BULL DESIGN

To my parents, Dick and Joan, for *not* monitoring my TV,

and

to brothers Tatsuo and Kenji Yoshida and Ippei Kuri for creating *Speed Racer*

CONTENTS

ACKNOWLEDGMENTS

A standing ovation to the individuals who shared their time, memories, and expertise, and who truly made *Speed Racer: The Official 30th Anniversary Guide* possible: Jerry Beck, Richard Brandt, Brian Buckley, Tony Caputo, Brian Carasik, Liane Curtis, Danny Davis, Peter Fernandez, Ron Fontenot, Howard Frank, Bill Goodell, Jack Grimes, Toshiko Hyakuno, Bobby Labonte, Fred Ladd, Mike Lazzo, Helen McCarthy, Maya McClure, Koki Narushima, Tim Neil, Corinne Orr, Fred Patten, Shelly Riss, Paulette Rubenstein, J. J. Sedelmaier, David Lane Seltzer, Linda Simensky, Jessica Suarez, Matthew Sweet, Michelle Talich, Neal Tiles, Dr. Treyzon, Kevin Triplett, Jimmy White, Anthony Williams, Pat Williams, Fred Wolf, Jimmy Yamasaki, and Kenji Yoshida.

I am also extremely thankful to my friends and family for their encouragement, love, and support, especially: Mom and Dad Moran, and my husband Valeriy Biktashev.

Finally, *Speed Racer: The Official 30th Anniversary Guide* wouldn't be possible if it weren't for Jim and John Rocknowski, Laurie Fox and Linda Chester, Bob Bull, and Laurie Abkemeier, Liz Kessler, David Lott, and Claudyne Bedell at Hyperion.

A big thank you to all of you!

FOREWORD

I did not create *Speed Racer,* nor did the original Japanese animators. It was created by children throughout the world — by almost every boy and girl who has ever played with toy cars. By most of us.

RRRooom, RRRooom, brrr — that was the sound of engines as we drove impossible courses around the floor, out on hard bare ground or soft sand. The crashes were spectacular but never disastrous. My car was never damaged, and no one was ever hurt.

When I was asked to adapt and direct *Mach Go Go Go* for English-speaking audiences, I remember screening the first episode and thinking that I had more than a challenge ahead of me — I had a job that was going to be fun!

From every episode there was something to learn, even about driving. Even today, I practice a few tips from the series. For instance, when approaching a sharp curve, I slow down. Halfway through the curve I gently accelerate. Better traction! Thanks, Speed.

Perhaps the most important and valuable lesson I learned from the *Speed Racer* series was that quality and integrity are a couple of the most important tips for traveling the road of life. Corinne Orr (Trixie/Spritle), Jack Grimes (Sparky/Chim Chim), and I poured everything we had into each episode. We gave it our all, and our best. Could that be one of the reasons the series has endured all these years?

— PETER FERNANDEZ (a.k.a. Speed Racer/Racer X)

"Huh? Oh!"

INTRODUCTION

Throughout my childhood, television viewing was neither restricted nor monitored in my family. Because my father sold commercial time for ABC-TV, watching television was almost encouraged. It was not a privilege, it was a right. It *mattered*. In fact, one of the first toys I recall playing with was a Fisher-Price windup television set that "broadcast" nursery rhymes.

I watched *a lot* of television.

Three moments vividly stand out in my mind from those early years. The first is the NBC Peacock. As if by magic, its black and white feathers changed into a rainbow of colored ones as the announcer proclaimed the upcoming show to be "brought to you in living color." Then there's *Bozo's Circus* bucket game where some lucky little kid from the audience was picked by a swiveling spotlight to play the beanbag toss game. And, finally, *Speed Racer* — specifically the theme song and the Mammoth Car episodes. I ran home to watch *Speed Racer*, fearing I would miss one second of the song.

Why *Speed Racer*?

I've spent much time pondering this very question, and during the course of writing this book I asked countless others for their opinions. Simply, *Speed Racer* was different. As a five-year-old in 1967, I couldn't articulate what made it different. But, instinctively, I recognized the show had qualities that set it apart from the animated fare of the time. Qualities that attracted me and legions of fans who, thirty years later, would elevate the

series to cult status, making it a symbol of our collective childhoods.

Speed Racer partisans seem to be those who were children in the 1960s. If you weren't devoted to the show then, it's likely you won't understand its popularity now. Interestingly, when the series was being prepared for broadcast on the Cartoon Network in early 1996, the general manager called the theme song "lame," suggesting that it be deleted from the program. Fortunately, the program director, an ardent fan of the show, prevented the ultimate sacrilege.

Hands down, the *Speed Racer* theme song is what is most fondly remembered about the series. The catchy, upbeat lyrics captured the essence of each exhilarating episode. The "grid" of race cars provoked curiosity, serving as a promissory note for more mind-boggling things to come. And the turn-of-the-century automotive parade, shown during the closing credits, still carries an air of mystery reminiscent of Racer X. Our seat belts were fastened. We were ready to roll with Speed over the most dangerous of terrains, defeating the most ruthless villains and, of course, winning races.

Arguably, *Speed Racer* wasn't the smoothest animation. Yet its stilted look did contribute to the overall effect. Creatively, the character development, art direction, plot, music, and effects were far superior to American animated shows of the 60s and early 70s such as *The Flintstones* and *Scooby-Doo*. Unlike the way we felt about these

American shows, we actually cared about Speed and his friends; we were genuinely concerned for their safety. In the sense that they expressed thoughts and feelings like our own, they were real. Also, Speed and his friends were characters we aspired to be. What kid didn't want to become a race car driver, a helicopter pilot, or a secret agent? Or, live in a functional and supportive household?

Speed Racer was not just a babysitter, a temporary distraction allowing a parent a little relief. Nor did it serve to fill our young vulnerable brains with useless garbage. Valuable life lessons were presented in each story. Lessons such as honesty, trust, selflessness, and courage. We learned the consequences of being selfish and greedy.

Although the inherent goodness of the show was masked by its excessive violence, it was *constructive* violence. The bad guys deserved what they got. The parameters of good and evil were clearly defined. Speed reciprocated a violent act only as a means of self-defense. Sadly, our parents and the governing bodies set up to police children's programming didn't see it that way. They didn't understand.

Speed Racer was also artistic. Reminiscent of a Disney theatrical release, it featured camera angles and sound and visual effects — depth that was not seen in American animated shows. In short, it was not "cartoony." Thankfully, it didn't have a laugh track or goofy music running continuously through the show. Instead, the thematic music and Hitchcockian camera angles were used to accentuate the action.

In the shadow of the Mammoth Car

Sunlight reflecting on the ocean is the kind of detail that set Speed Racer *apart from American animated cartoons.*

(Who can forget the sound the Mammoth Car made when it melted into a pool of gold?) In addition, the attention to detail was unsurpassed. Often, there were long takes on scenery — a sea gull gracefully gliding alongside the Mach 5, the sky reflecting in a mountain lake.

These qualities have made those of us who grew up with *Speed Racer* (and those who are just being introduced to the show) come back for more. In 1998, the original creators, Tatsunoko Production Co., Ltd., are set to release an all-new *Speed Racer* series worldwide.

This time, parents will understand. Because we are the parents.

Go, Speed Racer, Go!

— ELIZABETH MORAN

Speed's famous "go" position

"HERE HE COMES, HERE COMES SPEED RACER..."

The *Speed Racer* Theme Song

The lyrics to the American version of the *Speed Racer* theme song were written by Peter Fernandez, who also wrote and directed the voice-over for the series and provided the voices for Speed Racer and Racer X. This much is certain. Whether Peter wrote the lyrics to arranger Billy Mure's adaptation of the original Japanese theme or Billy arranged the music around Peter's lyrics is not clear. It was thirty years ago, and memories have faded.

Nevertheless, aside from Peter, four others were involved in creating the theme, although none received screen credit. First, Peter hired Danny Davis as producer. Peter and Jack "Sparky" Grimes knew Danny from working on a series of children's albums for MGM. Danny, in turn, hired arranger and musician Billy Mure. Danny also hired his boss at the time, manager of A&R in New York, Don Burkhimer (now general manager of Sony Music in Santa Monica, California), as vocalist. Danny and Don's secretary, Janet Leder-

man, also acted as vocalists. Together, Danny, Billy, Don, and Janet sang the theme. (A point of interest: Danny, Billy, and Don recorded two albums for RCA Records as The Palm Beach Band Boys. And today, Danny leads his band of twenty-nine years, Danny Davis and the Nashville Brass, winner of seven Country Music Awards and one Grammy.)

All in all, the one-minute-and-six-second theme, more than a minute shorter than its Japanese counterpart (2:13), was recorded in "one evening over a couple of hours," recalls Don. "We were paid $50 apiece." Chuckling, Danny disputes this, "It was more like $30." But why the difference in length? By shortening the theme song and making room for the pervasive commercials, the body of the show (for the most part) remained intact. Yet, the length of the Japanese version wasn't the only problem. Using the original music composed by Nobuyoshi Koshibe and translating its theme into English probably would not have worked. The pulse-pounding orchestration with its blaring brass section and chorus of male voices, all singing with great gusto, sounded more indicative of a military hymn than a cartoon. Billy Mure's upbeat, snappy rendition was more appealing to American sentiments.

Visually, two things differentiate the Japanese opening theme from the one we have come to love and know so well. The Japanese version begins with copy superimposed over a black screen and uses footage from various episodes, including a weird shot of Speed autojacking over the full-screen behinds of two elephants — a scene most likely taken from the "Crash in the Jungle" episode. The American version, conversely, stays with the racetrack sequence and the infamous "grid" of race cars. If you're interested in seeing the footage of the original Japanese opening, it is used in its entirety in the three-episode compilation film, *Speed Racer: The Movie*. If you want to hear the original Japanese audio, though, you'll probably have to scour the collectibles market, since the show is not currently syndicated in Japan. But finding this jewel is worth the effort in laughs!

Lyrics to the American Version of the *Speed Racer* Theme Song

Here he comes, here comes Speed Racer
He's a demon on wheels
He's a demon and he's going to be chasing after
  someone
He's gaining on you so you better look alive
He's busy revving up the powerful Mach 5
And when the odds are against him and there's
  daaaangerous work to do
You bet your life Speed Racer will see it
  through

Go Speed Racer
Go Speed Racer
Go Speed Racer goooo!

He's off and flying as he guns the car around
  the track
He's jamming down the pedal like he's never
  coming back
Adventure's waiting just aheeeeeaaaaad

Go Speed Racer
Go Speed Racer
Go Speed Racer goooo!

Frame from the opening theme song

Lyrics to the Japanese *Mach 5 Go Go Go* Theme Song

> Goh Mifune has come back with the Mach 5 to challenge in another race.

(Copy superimposed over a black screen.)

Go Mach 5 Go, go, go! (Title over spinning tire)
The white body of the Mach 5 zipping around a
  hairpin curve
Nothing can stop him, nothing can scare him
Go, go, gooooo!
With unyielding spirit, Goh Mifune drives the
  Mach 5
Once he starts driving, he is like a demon
He sees nothing other than the track
He gives everything to win

Go Mach 5, go
Go Mach 5, go
Go Mach 5, go, go!

The sharp-looking Mach 5. Goh Mifune
Step on the gas. Get more speed
Go Mach 5, speed up till the end of the earth
Young life flames in his heart
Go, go, goooo!
Watch his fearless spirit race
Speed up, speed up Mach 5 till the final victory

Go Mach 5, go
Go Mach 5, go
Go Mach 5, go, go!

Lyrics by Tatsuo Yoshida and Akira Ito; composed by Nobuyoshi Koshibe; vocals by Vocal Shop.

"Here He Comes, Here Comes Speed Racer. . ."

2

THE PIT CREW

"I've got to keep my head. I've got to stay calm!"

The Cast of *Speed Racer*

The characters in *Speed Racer* each play an integral role in the series. All are essential and partly responsible for helping Speed realize his dream as a world champion auto racer. In addition, each character summons a special memory, reminding us of our carefree childhood in which Speed's predicaments were our only concern. More often than not, we had to wait until the next day to see our hero conquer evil and win the race.

Speed Racer, Trixie, Spritle, Chim Chim, and the Mach 5

Speed Racer 三船　剛

For months I've been driving in races all over the world. There have been a lot of bad crashes and I've had some close calls. But the danger is a part of racing. Just as is the thrill of winning. I'll go on competing in races throughout the world because wherever there's a challenge, I've got to meet it.

Speed lives the good life — something most of us only dream about. Although he may be a cartoon character, Speed embodies all that so many of us wished for as eighteen-year-olds. Unencumbered by the effects of adolescence (not an ounce of baby fat or a blemish on this stud), Speed is remarkably at ease with his dynamic good looks, highlighted by gigantic baby blues that are rimmed with lush, girl-attracting lashes. Also, he was born into a family headed by a father who is the brains behind the most futuristic car in the world, the Mach 5. What kid wouldn't want to boast that at school?

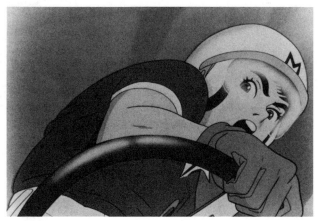

"OOOhhhhh!"

Although, in the beginning, Speed has to prove himself a responsible and capable driver, he soon wins his birthright to continue the family legacy. This lot fell to Speed after his older brother Rex ran away from home. As a professional driver, Speed continues to push himself, to prove that, indeed, he is worthy of the accolades bestowed on him at such a young age. And, like Spritle and Chim Chim, we are stowaways aboard the Mach 5. Ready to take on the most treacherous courses, we face the most ruthless villains with our hero as he competes in races around the world in such real-life destinations as Japan, Egypt, and Mount Rushmore, and other worldly places like Sandoland, Abalonia, and Flathill. We are there when he races blind or without brakes, when he sets a new land speed record or races the car no one could drive.

Ultimately, Speed does realize his dream of becoming the world's greatest race car driver, a title he earns "fair and square." However, winning races isn't his primary goal. Sometimes, he will intentionally lose a race to aid a total stranger, but more often, he will win a race while aiding the likes of Inspector Detector in whatever mysterious situation he encounters. What a guy! And, no matter what, Speed's girlfriend, Trixie, and his top mechanic, Sparky, are always nearby to lend a helping hand.

Racer X  三船　健一

Even though I am his brother, I can't go home again. I'm giving up being a racer. And from now on, I'll be a full-time international secret agent, without a name or country.

Undeniably, Racer X is the least understood driver on the Formula 1 racing circuit. Both feared and revered, he inspires rumors that whenever he competes, crashes are sure to occur. A face mask used to conceal his true identity further shrouds him in mystery, only adding to his reputation as a jinx.

Unbeknownst to Speed (and his family), Racer X is really his older brother, Rex Racer, a fact we are frequently reminded of throughout the series. Long ago, while competing in a race, Rex crashed a car Pops built. Subsequently, he ran away from home when Pops told him he lacked the necessary experience to race professionally. Aided by his mentor, Kabala, Racer X hones his driving skills, learning how to drive on "tortured roads and broken trails." After this internship, he becomes a professional driver.

The Shooting Star

Somewhere along the way, he adds "secret agent" to his resume. He uses his experience as a race car driver as cover for his primary occupation at the Paris-based International Police. Apparently, being a professional racer isn't enough for this thrill-seeker. While he keeps one eye on an array of criminals (seemingly all agents of International Spies, Incorporated) he keeps the other on Speed. Out of nowhere, Racer X appears to save his brother — and sometimes Spritle and Trixie — from dire circumstances. Soon, a mutual admiration develops between these two great rivals, and eventually Speed wonders if Racer X is his brother.

In the end, Racer X forsakes race car driving to become a full-time secret agent. No longer lured by fast cars, he turns his attention to the much more dangerous game of establishing world peace. However, he vows to an unconscious Speed that he'll "be near if you ever need help, no matter where you might go."

An emotional Speed, upon waking, sees the face mask his brother left behind. He declares, "Rex! Wherever you are, I promise to be the best racer in the world and to make you proud of your younger brother." And so he did.

The Pit Crew

Sprtle: 7 years, 11 months, 23 days and 8 hours old

Heading to the trunk!

Chim Chim

Sprtle 三船 くりお
and
Chim Chim 三平

"Sprtle's my name and mischief's my game."

For comic relief, there's none better than Speed's younger brother Sprtle and his pet chimpanzee, Chim Chim. Sprtle and Chim Chim are an inseparable team. They have a way

of popping up at just the right time to pull Speed out of a jam so that he can go on to save the day. They do this with the disconcerting habit of sneaking inside the Mach 5's trunk. It's amazing how this pint-sized pair is able to challenge and overcome muscle-bound thugs or gun-toting gangsters using slingshots, small rocks, and food as weapons. Yet, oftentimes, in an attempt to prove themselves to the family, they will try to solve a mystery on their own. Of course, their efforts only make matters worse. Packing as much slapstick punch as "The Three Stooges," these two love candy so much that they fight between themselves over whatever bribes they manage to collect. Needless to say, they eat a lot of candy!

Trixie 志村　ミチ

Trixie to the rescue!

TRIXIE: *I love taking the wheel.*

SPEED: *Take it easy! The speed limit through here is only 80 mph!*

TRIXIE: *Huh? Oh! I didn't realize we were going twice that fast. It drives so beautifully.*

Usually arriving in her helicopter, Speed's girlfriend

Trixie is always ready to aid Speed in a time of crisis. Whether performing search-and-rescue missions or smoke-bombing Speed's adversaries, Trixie never backs down in the face of danger. And, like Racer X, she happens to arrive just in the nick of time. She's one tough gal with enough spunk to keep up with her beau's high-octane adventures. She isn't afraid to speak her mind, either to Speed or to any of the villains she comes up against. Known to throw more than one surprised criminal for a loop, she'll do it again if fools cross her path. Loyal and protective, Trixie is direct and clear to Speed's female oglers and to various heads of state (who wish to betroth their daughters to Speed) that he is taken. After all is said and done, Trixie usually gets her way — even if she has to stow aboard the Mach 5.

"You know you won't win if you don't have me for an assistant."
— TRIXIE to SPEED

Sparky　サブ

I was just trying to find out if the Mammoth Car is equipped with any special inventions I don't know about.

Checkin' out the Mach 5

An integral part of the Mach 5 Go Team, ace mechanic Sparky is also Speed's best friend. Along with Pops, Sparky knows the Mach 5 inside and out. His job is to make sure the supercharged vehicle outperforms any other car on the track. Sometimes this means making last-minute adjustments, often seconds before the race begins.

Like the rest of Speed's support team, Sparky assists Speed off the track, also. Sometimes this requires him to put down his wrench and to put up his fists. His loyalty shines through when he does whatever it takes to help Speed, even finding him an essential auto part after being scolded by his

hero/friend. (Or is he more concerned about the Mach's welfare than Speed's?)

Also, he endeavors to improve the Mach 5. Motivated and curious, he's been known to snoop around a competitor's vehicle to get new ideas. Invariably, he gets into trouble. Sparky may not always be at Speed's side, but he's always behind the scenes, making things happen.

Pops Racer　三船　大介

Be a man, and don't let anyone know how afraid you are. It takes more courage to do that, Speed, than anything else.

The world's foremost automotive engineer, Pops Racer designed and built the fabulous Mach 5. Pops can always be counted on to be as loud and overbearing as any well-meaning father has the right to be. But his love for Speed and his faith in his son's ability as a top-notch race car driver brings out the kinder, gentler side of his personality, particularly in light of his overprotective treat-

ment of his first son, Rex. The older boy ran away from home when he was Speed's age. But this doesn't mean that Pops isn't protective of Speed. On occasion, Pops will battle many a villain, putting to good use his skills as a for-

Blowing a gasket

mer wrestling champion of the Westside Grunters and Groaners Club. Undoubtedly, his automotive genius, his enthusiasm (he was once hospitalized with exhaustion while outfitting the Mach 5 with winglets), and his advice help make Speed the superstar of the racing world.

Mom Racer 三船　アヤ

Now that you've quit your job, you won't know what to do with yourself. And I know how you like to keep busy. How about remodeling my kitchen, rebuilding the garage, and planting some shrubbery?

— MOM to POPS RACER

While Trixie depicts an independent, all-things-equal kind of woman (a harbinger of the Equal Rights Amendment), Mom Racer is her mirror opposite. She is the cookie-baking, June Cleaver goddess of the Racer homestead. Always there for her family, she is the true backbone of the Mach 5 Go Team. 'Nuf said.

Mom Racer, Domestic Goddess. She can whip up a batch of cookies in no time.

3

The Supercharged Formula 1 Mach 5 is an automotive machine incomparable to any other on the racing circuit. Its unique aerodynamic design, coupled with its special devices, makes this car the leader of a pack of little more than second-rate contenders.

The Mach 5: sleek, powerful star of the racing world

SPEED'S ULTIMATE DRIVING MACHINE
The Mach 5

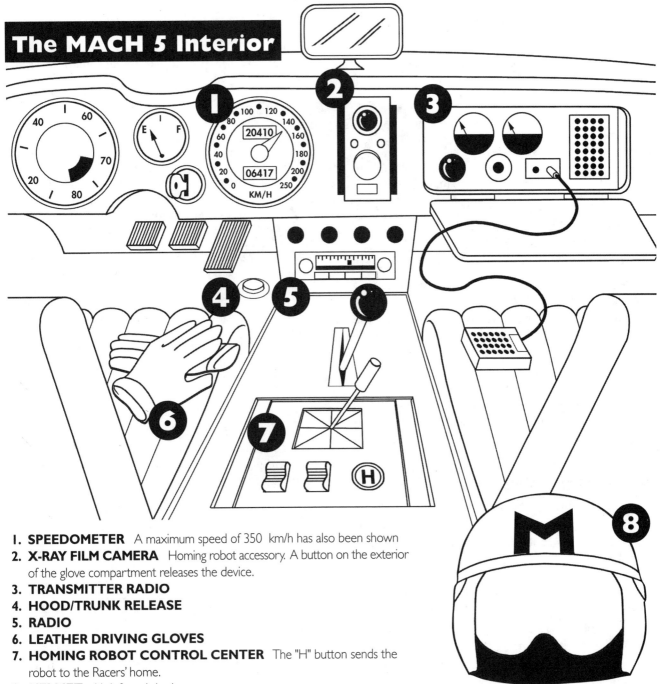

The MACH 5 Interior

1. **SPEEDOMETER** A maximum speed of 350 km/h has also been shown
2. **X-RAY FILM CAMERA** Homing robot accessory. A button on the exterior
   of the glove compartment releases the device.
3. **TRANSMITTER RADIO**
4. **HOOD/TRUNK RELEASE**
5. **RADIO**
6. **LEATHER DRIVING GLOVES**
7. **HOMING ROBOT CONTROL CENTER** The "H" button sends the
   robot to the Racers' home.
8. **HELMET** with infrared shades.

In episode 2, "The Great Plan," and again in episode 26, "The Car Hater," an overview of the Mach 5's control panel both enlightens and reminds us of the beauty of this truly remarkable machine. The hub of the Mach 5's steering wheel features seven lettered buttons, each of which activates a customized accessory designed by Pops Racer.

A close-up of the control panel

CONTROL A: "Releases powerful jacks to boost the car so that Sparky, our mechanic, can quickly make any necessary repairs or adjustments." Although designed for this practical function, the **auto jacks** have also been used to "leap" the car short distances at high speeds, as a wedge to prevent the car from toppling over a waterfall, as an alternative braking system, and as a tool to crush cars in a car wrestling match.

CONTROL B: "Sprouts special **grip tires** for traction over any kind of terrain. At the same time, 5,000 horsepower is distributed equally to each wheel by auxiliary engines." Definition of "any kind of terrain": firm, icy, or unsteady ground; ocean floor; vertical mountainsides.

CONTROL C: "For use traveling over heavily wooded terrain. Powerful **rotary saws** protrude from the front of the Mach 5 to slash and cut any and all obstacles." The rotary saws have also been used as a means of self-defense.

CONTROL D: "Releases a powerful **deflector** which seals the cockpit into an air-conditioned, bullet- and crash-proof, and water-tight chamber. Inside it, I am completely isolated and shielded." The deflector also protects against sleeping gas.

CONTROL E: "The control for **special illumination** which can be traversed singly or in tandem, and which enables me to see much farther and more clearly than with ordinary headlights. It's invaluable in some weird and dangerous places that I race the Mach 5." When used with the "night shades" attached to Speed's helmet, his vision is enhanced with infrared light.

CONTROL F: "Used when the Mach 5 is under water. First, the cockpit is supplied with **oxygen**. Then, a **periscope** is raised to scan the surface of the water. Everything that is seen is relayed down to me by **television**." The 100-pound auxiliary supply of oxygen is enough to last for thirty minutes.

CONTROL G: "Releases a **homing robot** from the front of the car. The homing robot can carry pictures or tape recorded messages to whomever or wherever I want to send them." The robot also can carry handwritten messages, X-ray film, rope, and small Egyptian statues, and it has been used as a means of defense. The bird-like device is operated by a built-in remote control within the cockpit. A separate button sends the robot "home."

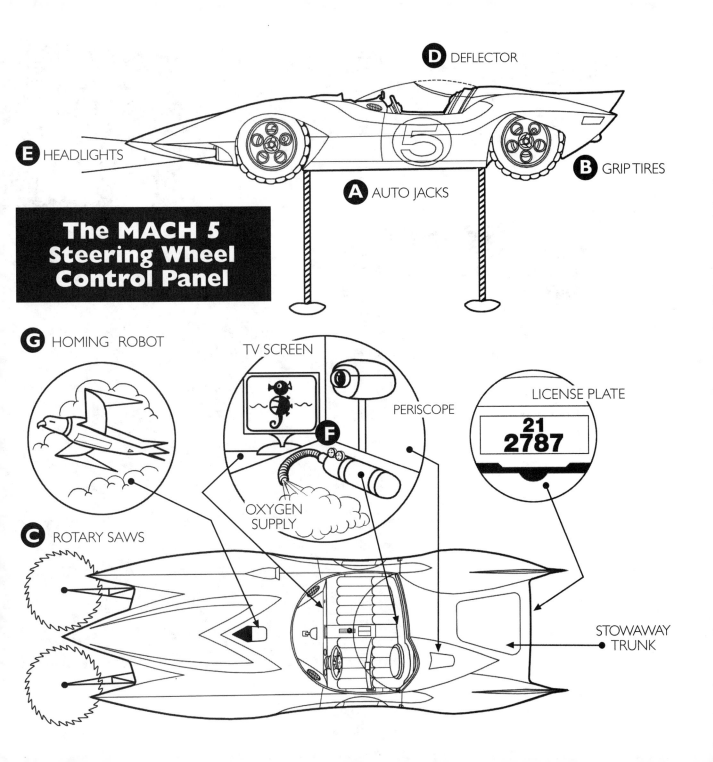

D DEFLECTOR

E HEADLIGHTS

B GRIP TIRES

A AUTO JACKS

The MACH 5 Steering Wheel Control Panel

G HOMING ROBOT

TV SCREEN

PERISCOPE

LICENSE PLATE

21
2787

F

OXYGEN
SUPPLY

C ROTARY SAWS

STOWAWAY
TRUNK

Jack 'er up!

The controls on the Mach 5 — the amazing car designed and built by my father. With this car, the most fabulous car ever driven, I've been competing in auto races throughout the world.
— SPEED RACER

RACE SPEAK

air dam *n.* Extension below front bumper of a race car that affects aerodynamics.

b-post *n.* Post extending from roof line to base of window behind driver's head.

binders *n.* Brakes.

black hat *n.* Driver who adopts a "bad" image; often wears black attire, drives a black vehicle. The Gang of Assassins are considered black hats.

deck lid *n.* Trunk lid.

drafting *v.* Occurs when one car follows another close behind; the first car cuts through the air and provides a cleaner pass for the car in back.

marbles *n.* Excess rubber build-up above upper groove on race track.

pole *n.* Inside position on the first row of the track. The winner on the first day of qualifying wins the pole position.

scuffs *n.* Tires with limited laps on them; most often used in qualifying.

spoiler *n.* Metal blade attached to rear deck lid of car; helps affect air flow over rear of car.

stickers *n.* New tires (that still have factory stickers on them).

tight *adv.* When front of car has difficulty turning corners.

last round of wedge *n.* Derived from the adjustment of the handling on the car by altering pressure on the rear springs.

white hat *n.* The opposite of black hat. Speed is a white hat.

4 START YOUR ENGINES!

The History of *Speed Racer*

In order to fully appreciate *Speed Racer*, one of Japan's most successful television imports, it is worth exploring just how Japanese animation, known as *anime* (AH-nee-may), came into existence.

Anime Past and Present

Long before the advent of film and television, Japanese artists passed down their folklore via narrative scroll painting. Once a popular art form in the medieval period, it eventually expanded over time, giving birth to *manga* (MAHN-gah) — comic strips and books. Early this century, with *manga*'s roots firmly established, Japanese artists looked west. They found new inspiration in animators Winsor McCay and Otto Messmer and, later, in brothers Max and Dave Fleischer and Walt Disney. European animators Jiri Trnka and Walerian Browczyk were also an influence. *Anime* was born. It didn't take long for westerners to sit up and take notice of this unique Japanese style.

Kitayama Seitaro's 1918 film, *Momotaro,* and Masaoka Kenzo's 1932 film, *Chikara To Onna No Yononaka,* Japan's first *anime* talkie, are only two examples of the plentiful and early work of *anime* pioneers.

Yet possibly the real force behind Japan's *manga* and *anime* industry is a man named Osamu Tezuka, known as the "God of Comics" (*Manga no kami-sama*) in his native country. As early as 1940, while still in school, Tezuka was already a prolific creator. According to Helen McCarthy in her book *Anime: A Beginner's Guide to Japanese Animation,* some 3,000 pages of his earliest *manga* survived World War II bombings. (By the time of his death in 1989, Tezuka is estimated to have drawn 150,000 pages of *manga*.) In 1946, at the end of the war, Tezuka at age seventeen made his comic debut with a newspaper strip, Ma-Chan's Diary. The next year, he produced his first solo *manga*. Its success elevated him to superstar status in the Japanese comic industry. Not one to shy away from any subject, Tezuka included in his *manga* works of science fiction, action/adventure, romance, and horror, earning fans of both sexes in every age group. Although he went on to complete a medical degree and become a licensed physician, *manga* appears to have been his true calling.

With the advent of television, Tezuka segued into *anime*, setting up his own production company, Mushi Productions. In 1962 he released his first *anime* film, an anthology called *Stories on a Certain Street Corner*. A year later, Tezuka delivered a true pioneer of Japanese television: *Tetsuwan Atom* (*Astro Boy*). Although not quite the first animated television series, it was the first series to have ongoing characters in a continuous story. *Otogi Manga Calendar* (1962), a series of disconnected shorts produced by the Otogi company, was the first animated television series. Nonetheless, Tezuka can be credited with originating Japan's first color animated series, known to westerners as *Kimba the White Lion* (*Jungle Taitei*).

When interviewed, McCarthy credited Tezuka's innate ability to combine Japanese idiom with Western influences as the reason for his work's popularity. "He incorporated many of the conventions of Western animation — the huge eyes (which were even popular back then), the distorted faces, and the way you could compress and stretch the body to express different emotions with Japanese folklore," says McCarthy. "If you look back at some of the sixteenth- and seventeenth-century woodcuts, you can see characters with these same distorted features. They are usually ghouls or other creatures, but the enormous eyes were seen as hypnotic and attractive. The eyes are the mirror into the soul." Conversely, Kenji Yoshida, president of Tatsunoko Production Co., Ltd. and *Speed Racer*'s original producer, when asked to comment on the use of oversized eyes, simply stated they were copying an American look. Nevertheless, for Tezuka to see how they were used in the West and then adapt them for his own work was a very important step. McCarthy continues, "It was the sort of step that took a genius like him to take and synthesize." With the success of Astro Boy and Kimba the White Lion, Tezuka demonstrated that there was an audience for animated TV fare. As a result, a whole crop of animation companies sprang up, including Tatsunoko.

Given Japan's infatuation with *manga*, it is not difficult to understand why the Japanese have embraced *anime*. Also, it is easy to see why *anime* appeals to Americans. In her outstanding *Film Quarterly* article, "Magical Girls and Atomic Bomb Sperm: Japanese Animation in America," Annalee Newitz offers insight into why both Americans and Japanese use *anime* as a window into their own worlds. "Watching *anime* gives Americans a chance to reflect on their own national culture in displaced form," she writes. "Although *anime* does often strike us as utterly different, it also quite noticeably resembles — and is influenced by — American mass culture and generic narratives. That Americans might be interested in looking at their own culture through Japanese eyes tells us that Americans' feelings about their own culture are deeply bound up with America's evolving relationship with Japan." She goes on to say that "the American occupation in Japan is still a topic very much alive in Japanese popular culture as both a manifest and a repressed theme."

In an attempt to help recover from the devastating effects of World War II, the Japanese have used *manga* and *anime* as a way of presenting parables of how best to move forward into the future. The popular robot genre (as well as the abilities of the Mach 5) offers a means to enhance man's power. Adds McCarthy, "*Manga* and *anime* have helped to encourage and maintain Japan's positive attitude toward technology, and by making it both popular and acceptable have thus contributed considerably to the nation's progress and prosperity."

Interestingly, Fred Wolf, who produced 1993's *The New Adventures of Speed Racer*,

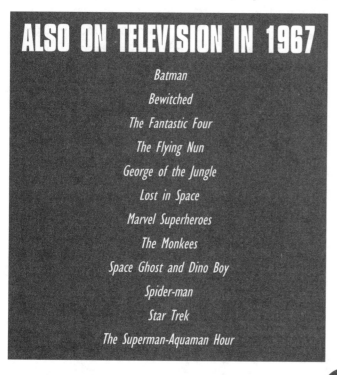

ALSO ON TELEVISION IN 1967

Batman

Bewitched

The Fantastic Four

The Flying Nun

George of the Jungle

Lost in Space

Marvel Superheroes

The Monkees

Space Ghost and Dino Boy

Spider-man

Star Trek

The Superman-Aquaman Hour

points out, "*Speed Racer* was the first show that empowered a kid, not on a superhero level, but on a more reality-based level." Set in exotic locales and filled with fast cars, adventure, and intrigue, *Speed Racer* managed to adapt the excitement and high technology of the robot story to a contemporary setting. Racing cars and flying helicopters is something a child can aspire to. In addition, while Mom Racer fulfilled the traditional role as domestic housewife and mother, Speed's girlfriend, Trixie, demonstrated that girls can share the same tier as their counterparts. In its own way, *Speed Racer* contributed to the women's movement, although according to Kenji Yoshida, this was not a conscious effort: "We didn't think about such things."

Anime Takes Root in the United States

Anime found its niche in the U.S. syndication market when NBC Enterprises (not to be confused with the NBC network) purchased the rights to *Astro Boy* in 1963, the same year the series made its Japanese debut on New Year's Day. Originally K. Fujita, the agent representing Mushi Productions (and later Tatsunoko), brought the series to the NBC network. But according to Fred Ladd, who wrote and directed the English adaptation of *Astro Boy*, "They wouldn't buy it. They didn't want to import shows from Japan or anywhere else because it wasn't worth it to buy a [foreign] show and then have to dub it into English. They wanted to create their own shows," he says. So, while the networks were paying production costs to domestic animation firms (Hanna-Barbera, by

*Note the poster in the background —
evidence of the cartoon's Japanese roots.*

this time, was in full swing producing *The Flint-stones*, *The Jetsons*, and *Jonny Quest*, among many others), *Astro Boy* established a marketplace for what the U.S. industry would tag "Japanima-tion." During the 1960s, *Astro Boy*, *Gigantor*, *Eighth Man*, *Kimba the White Lion*, *Marine Boy*, *The Amazing 3*, *Prince Planet*, and *Speed Racer* all made it onto American airwaves. According to Ladd, "The Japanese thought this was marvelous. They never dreamed that their little cartoons would be a big hit in America." In fact, it was icing on the cake. Yoshida recalls that at the time, none of their shows, or those of other Japanese anima-tion companies, were produced with the intention of distributing their product outside of Japan.

Nevertheless, Americans embraced these programs not for their quality but for the endearing characters and story lines. Furthermore, when considering quality, one must look to the fact that the *style* of Japanese animation is different from what is considered "traditional" animation. Fred Wolf explains, "In film, there are twenty-four frames per second. In traditional animation, each drawing is photographed two times for two frames (called on-two). So, if you have twelve drawings and you shoot two times, it would constitute twenty-four frames, cre-ating a fairly smooth look. But some-times you have to just shoot one drawing for one frame (called on-one). Many of Disney's things are on-one and it's superfluid. In Japan, they shoot each drawing three or four times, making it look more jerky or stilted. It was not a creative decision because no one wants it to look like that. They just thought they would get more for less."

Tatsunoko Production Co., Ltd.

Kyoto-born brothers Tatsuo (1933; he succumbed to cancer in 1978), Kenji (1935), and Toyoharu Yoshida (1940; he uses the pen name Ippei Kuri) founded one of Japan's leading animation studios, the Tokyo-based Tatsunoko Production Co., Ltd., in 1962. In Japanese, Tatsunoko means "sea-horse," hence the studio's seahorse cartoon emblem. This can be seen on the Mach 5's TV screen in episode 2, "The Great Plan, Part 2." It is also a

Tatsuo Yoshida with his children

Ippei Kuri
(a. k. a. Toyoharu Yoshida)

Kenji Yoshida

pun: Tatsu no co. translated is "Tatsuo's Company."

Tatsuo, himself, while still living in Kyoto at age twenty-one, was a self-taught comic artist. He worked as an illustrator for the local newspapers. In May 1954, he and his new bride moved to Tokyo after his good friend and fellow cartoonist, Mr. Koyama, convinced him that his talent could be put to better use in the more cosmopolitan city. Tatsuo found similar work illustrating children's magazines, but his income was barely enough to make ends meet. Soon he debuted his first magazine *manga*, a prowrestling series called "Tetsuwan Rikiya" and "Champion-Ta." His youngest brother, Ippei Kuri, recalls, "Almost overnight, he became well known throughout the [comic] industry."

A year later, at the age of fifteen, Ippei joined his brother to become his assistant. "Before I joined him, however, I was already burning with the desire to become a cartoonist. During my youth in Kyoto I purchased a few secondhand American comic books which had been discarded by the U.S. occupation forces. I was overwhelmed and strongly influenced by the character Superman — his robust physique and his macho appearance. In contrast, at the time, Japanese comic books were amateurish. I longed to design in the realistic style of the Americans."

However, under the tutelage of Tatsuo, his drawing became almost indistinguishable from his brother's. To separate their talent, Toyoharu adopted a pen name, Ippei Kuri. In 1956, Shimamura Publishing released his debut *manga*, a Pacific War–themed series called "Abarei Tengu." His other notable *manga* include "Z-Boy," "Missile Kintaro," "Mach Sanshiro," and "Ohzora Eh No Chikai." Ippei remembers, "One of my car-

Japanese logo for Mach Go Go Go

toon series caught the attention of the Shueisha publishing company. As a result, 'Z-Boy' became a serial in their monthly magazine. This was in June of 1957 and I was seventeen at the time. I had been recognized."

Yet Ippei had bigger aspirations. Early in 1962, he convinced his eldest brother to form an animation company. "We then plunged headlong into preparation of 'Z-Boy.' We were under contract with Toei Films and during the process of preparation, 'Z-Boy' had been revised and butchered so many times. Things did not go well with our first opportunity to break into television animation. Ultimately, the contract soured and we were released. It was then that we decided to go into the business of animation ourselves. Through newspaper ads we assembled a team of artists and animators from throughout Japan. We produced *Uchu Ace* (*Space Ace*) with high hopes that it would somehow find its niche in the mar-

A page from Tatsuo Yoshida's "Mach Go Go Go" manga

ketplace and, thusly, generate operating capital. But after putting the finishing touches on the first episode, we were still without a sponsor. It was a difficult period. We financed the production with our own money, money borrowed using our house and land as collateral. In addition, we turned our attention to drawing cartoons for magazines. With these earnings, we managed to stay afloat financially and to move ahead. It was our past experience as cartoonists that enabled us to weather the dips. And, when we were almost financially bankrupt, we received word that Fuji television would air our production."

Making its debut in May 1965, all fifty-two episodes of the black and white *Space Ace* were broadcast weekly on Channel 8, Fuji TV, ending April 1966. Tatsunoko's second series, and its first color series, *Mach Go Go Go* (*Speed Racer*), debuted a year later on the same network. Also fifty-two episodes (roughly half are two-part serials), the series aired weekly at 6:30 P.M. from April 2, 1967, to March 31, 1968.

Ippei remembers, "*Mach Go Go Go* was based strictly on our all-out adoration of America. A defeated people witnessed American GI's riding about comfortably in their jeeps. American movies showed a life of abundance in the average household. Refrigerators were stuffed with food and fresh milk. It was absolutely unbelievable, like the Superman comics."

It should be noted, however, that *Mach Go Go Go* actually began as a series of *manga* created

by Tatsuo and published by Sun Publishing. At the time, Tatsuo decided to follow what was being done already on TV — adapting a popular *manga* to *anime* (*Astro Boy*, *Gigantor*, and *Eighth Man* all began as *manga*). Consequently, even though Tatsuo conceptualized *Mach Go Go Go* as an original TV cartoon, he published the story as a

The mysterious letters finally explained

comic first with the intention of promoting the *anime* adaptation as "based on the popular *manga*," as had been done with the others.

Middle brother Kenji points out, "Not many people know this, but the 'Mach Go Go Go' *manga* is based on another of my brother's *manga* called 'Pilot Ace.' It was also about a car, and the characters were similar to those in *Mach Go Go Go*. The 'Mach Go Go Go' *manga* was well received and we decided to adapt it to television. Also, at the time, auto racing was pretty popular in Japan."

Working jointly with an intermediary agency (Yumiko Productions), Tatsunoko went into pre-production with Channel 4, Nippon TV. "We did all kinds of color testing," Kenji recalls. "We weren't sure if we were going to produce the show in black and white or color. Only a third of the

people had color TV. And the color was not as good as it is today, so we took a lot of time testing. All of a sudden, our agency said that we changed TV stations to Channel 8, Fuji TV, and they agreed to pay for the show. Oftentimes an episode wasn't completed until the day before air."

Although not a big hit, *Mach Go Go Go* was popular because "there weren't many cartoons on

TV," Kenji explains. "Animation on TV was still new, so people watched. But maybe *Mach Go Go Go* was too American for the Japanese audience. It didn't talk to their hearts like *The Adventures of Hutch, The Honeybee.* Now that was a hit." However, *Mach Go Go Go* was successful enough to garner a toy deal. In fact, recalls Kenji, "The *Mach Go Go Go* model kit was second only to the best-seller model kit of the Ford Thunderbird."

Speed Racer Makes Tracks to the United States

The Japanese title, *Mach Go Go Go,* is a bilingual pun. *Go* in Japanese means "5" and the American phrase, "go, go, go!" Speed's Japanese name is Goh Mifune (Tatsuo Yoshida paid homage to the character, naming his first son Goh): The G on his racing tunic stands for Goh, and the M on his helmet is for Mifune Motors (understandably, the American audience assumes the M stands for Mach 5). The M on Trixie's blouse stands for her Japanese name, Michi Shimura. Curiously, these letters are never explained in the American adaptation. Why Peter Fernandez, who wrote, directed, and provided the voices for Speed and Racer X, didn't choose a name reflecting the letters remains a mystery. Fernandez recalls, "Naming the characters was fun. Speed was an obvious name, but I couldn't think of one for his older brother, so he became Racer X. Pops, Sparky, and Chim Chim were easy. Trixie was a cute name I made up. And Spritle was sprite."

(For years his name has been misspelled Spridle, Spridal, or Spridel.)

Coincidentally, the S on Sparky's T-shirt does reflect his Americanized name; his Japanese name being Sabu. For the record, Spritle's Japanese name is Kurio; Chim Chim is Sanpei; Racer X is Kenichi (after Kenji Yoshida); Mom and Pops are Aya and Daisuke Mifune; and Inspector Detector is Rokugo Keibu.

In 1967, roughly a year after *Mach Go Go Go* broadcast in Japan, K. Fujita, the same agent who sold *Astro Boy* to NBC Enterprises, brought the series to the United States. Initially, Fujita offered the show to Fred Ladd, who already had a reputation dubbing foreign cartoons into English. (He produced, wrote, and directed the English adaptations of *Astro Boy*, *Gigantor*, and *Kimba the White Lion*, among others.) "If I had been smarter, I would have bought it," remembers Ladd, "but my partner had just died. I always knew that *Speed Racer* would be big." Ultimately, *Speed Racer* was purchased by New York-based Trans-Lux Television Corporation (who distributed *Gigantor* for Ladd).

Known for its rear screen projectors (*trans lux* in Latin means "through light" — rear screen projection projects light through the screen to the audience), the company developed its entertainment division when it acquired a series of educational films produced by Encyclopedia Britannica in the late 1950s. Then, Trans-Lux collaborated with Joe Oriolo, the Paramount animation artist who developed *Casper the Friendly Ghost*, to produce a series of four-minute *Felix the Cat* cartoons for television. (The character was originally created by Pat Sullivan, Otto Messmer, and John King as an adjunct to the Paramount Screen Magazine newsreel in 1919.) Syndicated in 1960, *Felix* was followed by *The Mighty Hercules* in 1963, also produced and directed by Oriolo.

To adapt *Mach Go Go Go* for an American audience, Trans-Lux contracted with editors Pablo Zavala and Shelly Riss (Zavala-Riss) to do the job. Although broadcast in Japan on 35mm, the series aired on 16mm in the United States. Only the net-

works broadcast on 35mm. Zavala-Riss contacted Peter Fernandez to write and direct the adaptation. Fernandez hired the other voice actors: Corinne Orr (Trixie, Spritle, Mom Racer), Jack Grimes (Sparky, Chim Chim), and Jack Curtis (Pops, Inspector Detector). He found band leader

Danny Davis, whom he knew from MGM Children's Records, to produce a new version of the Mach Go Go Go theme song. "We were like a little band of dubbers in New York," Shelly Riss recalls. Asked if he had to tone down *Speed Racer*'s vio-

Examples of Speed Racer's *excessive violence*

lence, Riss states, "You can get away with a lot more in syndication. We edited for time and content." Incidentally, Zavala-Riss, Titra (where the voice-over was recorded), and Fred Ladd all maintained offices at 1600 Broadway in New York.

Around 1969, according to Richard Brandt, CEO of Trans-Lux, "We decided that being in the children's programming syndication business was not the best idea for the future. We sold most of our library to Alan Gleitsman (Alan Enterprises).

In those days, there were not a lot of TV stations to get on. So, when we syndicated to the local stations that were network affiliates, they said that the networks were insisting they put on *their* shows." By the mid-1970s, the influx of American-made cartoons simply forced Japanimation off the air.

In addition, standards for children's programming were becoming more strict. Organizations like the PTA, *Parents Magazine,* and certain other antiviolence groups specifically denounced Japanimation. An episode of *Speed Racer,* "The Car Hater," is a good example of what these groups deemed unacceptable. In this episode, a man seeks to avenge his son's death after a car accident. To prove how dangerous automobiles are, he hires a couple of thugs to tamper with the brakes on several race and street cars. In one scene, he beats his daughter with a horsewhip for admiring the Mach 5. Ultimately, the father causes an accident in which his daughter almost dies. Although he repents in the end, the damage has been done — literally. Unfortunately, the action and violence in *Speed Racer* and other Japanimated shows are so inherent to the story that they are impossible to edit. Finally, the modest number of episodes keeps *Speed Racer* from enjoying perpetuity on U.S. airwaves. Fifty-two episodes is well short of what is required for syndication.

Because of these reasons, *Speed Racer,* for the most part, left commercial television. In 1981, Alan Gleitsman renewed his license with Tatsunoko, later selling his entire library (including

Speed Racer) to Color Systems Technology in 1986 (Color Systems was known for colorizing films). From here, ownership of *Speed Racer* passes through many hands. By 1989, Color Systems Technology went bankrupt. General Electric Pension Trust, Color Systems' lender, held the library as security. That same year, Broadway Video, owned by Lorne Michaels (creator and producer of *Saturday Night Live*), bought the library from the Trust. In 1992, John Rocknowski acquired the rights to *Speed Racer* and established Speed Racer Enterprises, based in Santa Monica, California.

Formerly the Director of Marketing for Mattel, John Rocknowski has long been familiar with the merchandising arena. In 1972, after he left the toy giant, he and a partner set up a company to license American products in Japan. "And it only made sense to turn around and sell Japanese prop-

erties in America, and in other places around the world," he states. "In 1978 I met with Tatsunoko and acted as an agent for them, but this didn't have anything to do with *Speed Racer*. In fact, later, I also met with Alan Gleitsman because I was interested in handling just the merchandising, but there wasn't potential there at the time. And when I read that he sold the show, I told Tatsunoko, but they just let it happen."

Given the legal entanglements that began after Gleitsman sold his library, it's a wonder anyone was able to secure a license for Speed Racer. However, perseverance does pay off. Tony Caputo, founder of NOW Comics, and David Lane Seltzer are two examples. The latter, a senior at Harvard University in 1986, realized *Speed Racer*'s potential to be a blockbuster movie hit. "I was watching Top Gun and the scene where Tom Cruise puts on his helmet in the cockpit reminded me of Speed Racer," David recalls. "So, from my dorm, I set about tracking down the rights. I got to Alan Gleitsman, then to John Rocknowski, and eventually to Tatsunoko. I optioned the rights from Tatsunoko for

Life-size Mach 5 built by Tatsunoko for a press conference debuting the new Mach Go Go Go *in Japan*

one dollar. Then, upon graduation, a friend of mine gave me an office at Universal. I thought Richard Donner and Joel Silver (of Lethal Weapon and Superman fame) would be perfect to do the film, so I set up a pitch meeting with them at Warner Bros. and in 1989 we made a deal to become partners. The rights were transferred and they renewed the option."

"This is where I come in," recalls Rocknowski. "I remember Tatsunoko telling me about the film option with David. I was still not involved with *Speed Racer* at this point. Anyway, in 1990, Ippei Kuri (who was president of Tatsunoko at the time) and Executive Managing Director Koki Narushima (who also acted as translator) were in Los Angeles to meet with Warner Bros. They asked if I could come along and talk for them. We walked into this big Hollywood meeting. Donner is very enthusiastic and continues to repeat how he loves the concept and that he wants to make three movies. But he says Warner has a problem because Broadway Video has all the licensing rights for the animation. So, what WB wanted was for Tatsunoko to turn over all rights to them. Kuri and Koki looked at me. We said absolutely not." Rocknowski explained that he and Tatsunoko would not relinquish control. Rather, they would handle the legal matters, including clearing all rights in question. "Before Kuri left town, he asked me if I would be Tatsunoko's consultant for a while. By the end of the year, I told them that the potential for this property was too big to work on a part-time basis. The only way I could continue working on it was if I could buy the rights and work full time." With his son, Jim, they've managed to turn the property into a business generating revenue exceeding $50 million.

As of this writing, *Speed Racer: The Movie* is still in "active development." Having gone through a myriad of writers, a script has not yet warranted a green light for production. Nevertheless, many celebrities have either been discussed or have expressed interest in the project, including Johnny Depp, Nicholas Cage, Charlie Sheen, Chris O'Donnell, and Tom Cruise. "This movie *will* get done," Seltzer exclaims.

Apart from the feature film, Speed Racer has had success on cable television. In March 1993, MTV broadcast the show (although they only contracted to air twenty-six out of the fifty-two episodes). Its success prompted an updated 90s version, The New Adventures of Speed Racer, produced specifically for syndication by Fred (Teenage Mutant Ninja Turtles) Wolf. *Speed Racer*'s universe has expanded even more with its debut on the Cartoon Network in February 1996. In addition, Speed Racer has been the subject of commercial campaigns by Volkswagen GTI and NASCAR, both produced in 1996.

However, the most exciting prospect will not be seen by an American audience until 1998. On Thursday, January 9, 1997, at 7 P.M. on Channel 12 (Tokyo Broadcast System), Tatsunoko debuted the first of fifty-two episodes of the all-new *Mach Go Go Go*.

With an abundance of ongoing merchandising deals and the feature film and translation of *Mach Go Go Go* on the horizon, we Americans can be assured that *Speed Racer* will be around for new generations of fans to enjoy

5

LISTEN UP!

The Voices of *Speed Racer*

For years we've seen their names scroll by on *Speed Racer's* credits. But who are Peter Fernandez, Corinne Orr, Jack Grimes, and Jack Curtis? They're the actors who provided the voices for the characters. They are also talented individuals, each with impressive backgrounds. Interestingly, the roles they played thirty years ago have propelled them to cult superstardom. Meet the people whose names have become as familiar as our own.

Peter Fernandez: Speed Racer and Racer X

Despite it having been thirty years since Peter Fernandez wrote and directed *Speed Racer* and provided the voices for both Speed and Racer X, at age seventy, he still *sounds* like Speed Racer. His slightly raspy voice and clipped intonation are unforgettable, having formed an indelible impression in the minds of all who have watched the show. "Now, I have to reach up for Speed's voice. I'm closer to that of Racer X," Fernandez admits.

Born in Manhattan on January 29, 1927,

Peter is the oldest of three children. His father, a Cuban whose family came from Spain, headed an import-export firm and married his secretary Edna, Peter's mother. After the business became a casualty of the Depression, Peter, at age seven, helped his family make ends meet as a John Robert Powers model. "My mother saw an advertisement on the subway with some kid on it and she thought, 'Somebody must be doing that.' I met Mr. Powers and right away he started sending me out. I was just about in every ad that had a little boy in it."

Four years later, he segued into acting. Without prior experience, he landed a part on Broadway in *Whiteoaks* with none other than the grande dame of theater, Ethel Barrymore. "We did the national tour all over the United States and Canada. And we became the first summer package of a play with the cast intact." The lead in William Saroyan's *Love's Old Sweet Song* followed. In total, Peter performed in seven Broadway plays.

In between plays and his work at the Professional Children's School, Peter performed in over a thousand live radio shows. "Sometimes five or six in a day," he recalls. They included *The Aldrich Family*, *The Greatest Story Ever Told*, *Let's Pretend*, and many of the daily soap operas, including *Just Plain Bill* and *Snow Village*.

The day after he graduated from high school, he was drafted into the army. "That spring, thank God, the war ended in Europe. We were being trained to take part in the invasion of Japan and felt a great sense of relief and joy when the atom bomb saved us from going." Instead, while his troop was sent to Germany, Peter was transferred to the Pentagon where he worked as a mail clerk. Later, he was given a job as an announcer for the U.S. Army Band radio show.

After completing his sixteen-month duty, Peter resumed his acting career in a road production of *Pick Up Girl*. In 1949, now twenty-one years old, he secured the lead in the film *City Across the River*. "Bernie Schwartz was in it, but he got credited as Anthony Curtis. In his biography, there's a picture of me. And he writes, 'Due to obstinacy and stupidity of the director, they didn't cast me in the lead. And where are Peter Fernandez and (he named another fellow in the movie) now?' And in capital letters he says, 'DOWN THE TOILET OF NO RETURN.' I've always been tempted to write him a friendly letter with the return address of Toilet of No Return."

During his army stint, Peter had developed an affinity for writing. He first published, in an army magazine, a poem called "Oh That PX Beer." "I wrote about the hangover, of course." He went on to write many radio and television programs during the 50s, including *Right to Happiness* and *Suspense* for radio, and *The Verdict Is Yours* and *Rendezvous* for CBS-TV.

In 1950 he married actress Marian Russell. They bought a farm in Bucks County, Pennsylvania, and adopted two children. Unfortunately, because of their heavy work schedules and the arduous commute, the marriage came to an end after fourteen years.

Around 1963, a company called Titra hired him to write, direct, and dub voices into English for foreign films. "I'd get a very rough translation. And you would have to cover every little twitch to make it look like it was filmed in English." Some of his credits include the Japanese cult-classic "Godzilla" films, *Astro Boy,* and *Gigantor.* He also dubbed some Egyptian films starring a young Omar Sharif.

At this time, and for the next twelve years, Peter directed and sometimes adapted hundreds of children's books for schools and libraries. In 1967, Zavala-Riss, the editing company, hired him to prepare *Speed Racer* and *Marine Boy* for syndication in the English-speaking market. Did he think the series would be elevated to cult status some thirty years later? "Nope. It was just another job. Now, I get a wonderful reaction. People are very excited that they actually get to meet Speed Racer."

Since *Speed Racer,* some of his writing/directing credits include *Ultraman* (syndicated, 1968), *Star Blazers* (syndicated, 1979), *Galaxy Rangers* (syndicated, 1986), and, for the Fox network, *Princess Gwenevere and the Jewel Riders* (1996). He has also served as announcer in a myriad of television and radio commercials.

For the past nineteen years, Peter has been married to Noel Smith, a writer and poet. They live in Rockland County, New York, along with a number of cats, chickens, ducks, Canada geese, "and anything else that wants to move in." As his hobby, Peter haunts flea markets and auctions to add to his collection of antique toy banks.

Corinne Orr: Trixie, Spritle, and Mom Racer

In 1967, syndicated columnist Earl Wilson wrote, "You may not get straight answers when you talk with Corinne Orr, but you'll get a lot of laughs." Thirty years later, his statement holds true. Corinne's rapid-fire speech and sparkling personality reflect the children's cartoon voices she has provided over the years.

Now in her late fifties, Corinne was born in Montreal. Her father, a tailor, and her mother, an artist, had three children. Corinne is the youngest. Until age five, her family lived in the small French-Canadian town of St. Hyacinthe. Then they moved to an upper-class, English-speaking section of Montreal "where we lived beyond our means," Corinne reflects. "I had a funny French accent and the kids would laugh at me. My mother sent me for elocution lessons and I was hooked. I ended up doing a lot of children's theater beginning at age ten. That's where I started developing my cartoon voices." Corinne's expanding family proved to be as much a training ground as her theater experience. An aunt at age nine and a great-aunt at thirty, she admits to "stealing their voices." "I had a great rapport with kids."

As a youngster, Corinne became a member

of the Montreal Repertory Theatre and Montreal's Mountain Playhouse ensemble, acting alongside Christopher Plummer ("before anyone knew who he was") and William (*Star Trek)* Shatner. A few years later, around 1960, she landed a three-year stint as Suzie Mouse on the children's soap opera *Chez Helene*, a bilingual program devoted to teaching children English and French. "At that time Bob Goulet and I were the two top-paid performers. I made about $7,000. It was a lot of money back then."

Several years after that, Corinne moved to New York City. With only $1,000 in her pocket, she unpacked at the famed Barbizon Hotel for Woman. "It was so exciting. I was from a strict upbringing, and being on my own was magical." Although she can't recall her first job in the Big Apple, she does remember working regularly on the daytime soap opera *The Nurses* ("I would get the disease-of-the-week"). Many television and radio commercials and programs followed.

In 1966, Corinne worked for a short time as a "slater" at Titra, the company that dubbed foreign movies into English. A year later, she segued into voice-over work. Since she could do children's voices, she became the "resident kid." "Sometimes they would throw me a real part. From there, I did a lot of cartoons." Some of her cartoon credits include *Star Blazers, Ultraman, Marine Boy,* and *Speed Racer,* in which she played Trixie and Spritle. "I worked day and night and I took typing on the weekends because my father was sick and I had to send money home."

Since *Speed Racer,* Corinne has continued working as a voice-over actress. In addition to commercials and cartoons, she narrates children's stories, has provided voices for several dolls (the kind with the pull string on the back), and, occasionally, records statistical reports for financial corporations. For the past thirteen years, she has been the voice of Snuggle the Bear on the Snuggle fabric softener commercial. "I auditioned with about four hundred people. They took three to four months to pick me.

"My funniest audition happened when I got a call and they needed me for a baby cry. I was on Fifth Avenue at a phone booth and I told them I couldn't do it on the street. But they said they needed it now. So I started to cry. *Everyone* on the street stared, but I got the job."

Highly regarded in her field, Corinne still is very much sought after, both professionally and by her fans. Every week, invariably, she receives a letter from someone seeking advice on how to "get into the business." Her answer is to first take acting lessons. "I can do a voice I did twenty years ago. I have a good ear and I can remember where the voice came from. Sometimes it's head. Other times it's chest and/or nasal. Spritle is harder because it's throatier." Her other trick-of-the-trade is to eat a lot of hard candy "to get the saliva going." "Also, chewing gum helps you articulate."

Single, Corinne has lived on the upper east side of Manhattan for the past twenty-five years. An avid mineralogist, she belongs to the Mineralogical Club of New York at the Museum of Natural History.

Jack Grimes: Sparky and Chim Chim

Jack Grimes was born in Manhattan on April Fool's Day, 1926. But as a youngster, he had little time to fool around. In the midst of the Depression and before the present system of welfare was implemented, families banded together. When Jack's father lost his job as a carpet maker at Gimbel's department store, Jack, at age ten, helped support his parents, two siblings, and the two cousins who had joined their close-knit Irish family.

"I had a normal childhood until I was about seven-and-a-half," Jack remembers. "I was very bright. I could read and write. And I wasn't afraid of anything or anybody. A neighbor of mine, who was in vaudeville, read in *Variety* that they were casting for a [Broadway] play, *Old Maid* with Judith Anderson and Helen Menken. He asked my parents if he could take me down there, and I went in to read for it. I got the part. The play won a Pulitzer Prize and ran for ten months in New York. Then we went on tour for eleven months." His salary was $25 a week. His father had earned $9 a week.

Jack acted in several more plays, including *Excursion* with Shirley Booth. Backstage, Jack met Nila Mack, creator, writer, and director of the CBS children's radio program, *Let's Pretend*. She asked him to audition. Arthur Anderson chronicles the show in his book, *Let's Pretend: A History of Radio's Best Loved Children's Show by a Long-time Cast Member*. Anderson recalls, "Of all the Pretenders, Jack Grimes was the most successful in his radio career. During the years 1937 to 1946, Jack (and another Pretender) probably played close to ninety percent of the male child parts in New York radio." Jack played a "Pretender" for eighteen years until the show went off the air in 1954.

Other than *Let's Pretend*, Jack was cast in a host of radio shows, including *Fred Allen*, *The Phillip Morris Playhouse*, *Second Husband* (for nine years), and *Death Valley Days*. "Since I was about twelve, I was doing between thirty-five and forty radio shows a week."

That didn't leave much time for school. In fact, his lack of attendance caught up with him. After the eighth grade, he left the Professional Children's School to join the Lodge Tutoring School. "It was in [the teacher's] apartment, and I would go to see him and tell him what shows I was doing. He would tell me what chapter to do, and then I would come back the next day and he would quiz me. That's how I did four years of high school in two-and-a-half years." In 1942, at age sixteen, Jack entered Columbia University, taking courses in history and law.

In 1944, Jack enlisted in the air force. Big-band leader Glenn Miller was to be his commanding officer. However, because of his small stature ("I was like five feet two inches and ninety-two pounds at the time"), he was soon discharged.

The big screen called. In 1944, Jack commuted to California to act in a few films produced by Universal: *Fairytale Murder*, *Lady on a Train*, and *Weekend at the Waldorf*. "CBS [Radio] was very good to me," he recalls. "They would replace me on the radio shows so I could come out and do these movies." Soon after, in 1949, at age twenty-three, he married Joan Farrell. Anderson writes, "When Jack asked Joan's father for her hand in marriage, Mr. Farrell wanted to know how much money Jack made. Jack, knowing that a nonperformer would never understand our unpredictable income, quoted the AFTRA overtime rehearsal rate, six dollars an hour, which at that time was an excellent wage. Hearing that, Joan's father decided not to raise any objections."

In the 50s, Jack had no trouble making the transition from radio to television. Some of his early appearances include *Alcoa Presents*, *Love of Life*, *The Aldrich Family*, and *Tom Corbett, Space Cadet*. But, for those who watched *Speed Racer*, he probably would be best remembered for *Maude*, *On the Rocks*, and *All in the Family*. (For the latter, he received an Emmy nomination for the role of Mr. Whitehead, the undertaker.) "When I was doing *All in the Family*, we would be presented to the audience before the show. One day, someone got up and said they knew my voice and asked if I had done *Speed Racer*. Carroll O'Connor turned to me and said, 'What the hell is *Speed Racer?*'"

Although Jack and Peter Fernandez had crossed paths as youngsters, it wasn't until 1962 "that we renewed our acquaintance." Hired by MGM to produce and direct a series of records, Jack hired Peter as a writer. Five years later, Peter would cast Jack as the voice of Sparky and Chim Chim in *Speed Racer*. "The day after we finished the series I had to fly to the West Coast to do a movie called *Pendulum* with George Peppard." *Cold Turkey* with Dick Van Dyke followed in 1971.

By 1986, Jack "had had it [with show business]. A friend of mine, who was a district attorney, needed PR help and I asked him to hire me. So I worked for the Queens' borough DA for five years."

Ironically, Jack claims he never really enjoyed "doing over twelve thousand radio shows, six plays, half a dozen motion pictures, and about two hundred TV shows" in his career. If he had to do it over again, he would be a lawyer — "probably."

Jack and his wife of forty-eight years still live in New York. They have three children and five grandchildren.

Jack Curtis: Pops Racer and Inspector Detector

A mere three years after Speed Racer made its American television debut in 1967, Jack Curtis, age forty-four, met an untimely death from liver disease. However, the baritone voice behind Pops Racer and Inspector Detector lives on, helping to create legions of Speed Racer fans.

Born in New York on June 16, 1926, Jack was an only child. His father, also named Jack, had emigrated from Latvia. Not until he joined a vaudeville act called The Flying Curtis Brothers did he legally change his name from Zinn to Curtis. Later, he would step out of the limelight to become a theatrical agent. Jack Jr.'s mother, Mabel Ford, came from a show business background also. Raised in Covington, Kentucky, Mabel was the youngest of The Four Dancing Fords (comprised of two sisters and two brothers). Famous for clog dancing, the four siblings would perform in unison, followed by solo pieces. Reportedly, a scientist even tried unsuccessfully to calculate how fast their feet moved. From around 1902 to 1915, the troupe was heralded as one of the top vaudevillian performers, traveling extensively in the United States and in Europe.

When Jack Jr. was born, his father had little patience with him. He was ashamed of his son's damaged left hand and took him to countless doctors. "Jack was born without all his fingers," recalls Jack Jr.'s second wife, Paulette. "Apparently, the umbilical cord wrapped around his hand, stunting its growth." Unfortunately, the stigma remained with him throughout his life. Corinne Orr remembers, "Jack would hide his hand in his pocket."

However, his misfortune did not deter him. At a young age, he began piano lessons. Having an ear for music, he quickly was able to repeat everything he heard. Later, as a teenager in the 1940s, Jack got into voice acting. He performed on a myriad of radio shows, including *Coast to Coast on a Bus,* where he first met Peter Fernandez.

Some time in the mid 1950s, he met and married Terry Van Tell. Terry was chosen as a contestant on the first prime-time television game show, *The $64,000 Question.* Terry won more than the $64,000 prize (it remains a mystery if she was one of the contestants for whom the show's staff provided answers — a common practice that was done secretly as a ratings booster), and the money funded Jack's aspiration to get into the film business. In 1964, Jack made what is now considered a cult classic, *The Flesh Eaters,* his first and only endeavor. Although Jack is credited as its director, he also wrote, provided the camera work, and edited the film.

Sadly, Jack's marriage to Terry was short-lived. Later, while employed at the New York dubbing company Titra, he met his second wife, Paulette Rubinstein, who worked as a voice-over actress and dubbing director. They married on

New Year's Eve, 1963. A daughter, Liane, was born in 1964. Soon after, his longtime friend Peter Fernandez hired him to dub *Speed Racer* and provide voices for the *Marine Boy* series.

Although Jack may have been self-conscious about his physical handicap, he more than made up for it with his humor. "He spoke in non sequiturs," Corinne recalls. "I think his brain was so fast, he was ahead of what he was telling you. I was one of the few who understood him." Always one for a practical joke, "he would go into a restaurant and order a shrimp and peanut butter sandwich. The waitress would ask if he was sure. Then, he would come back the next week and they would give him the sandwich and he would say, 'What kind of stupid sandwich is this? No one in their right mind would eat this!' He was very funny."

Peter Fernandez recalls that Jack directed an antismoking commercial for television, and Jack hired him as the actor even though they were both heavy smokers.

In fact, "When he gave up smoking, he sucked on a baby pacifier. When people would stare, Jack would suck on it even more. He was so outrageous, and a warm and giving person," Corinne recalls. Paulette, now remarried, agrees, "He was a tough act to follow."

52 LAPS AROUND THE TRACK

The Complete *Speed Racer* Episode Guide

SPEED RATINGS

Speed Racer episodes have been scored with a rating system from 1 to 5 Mach 5 cars. Each score was determined by plot complexity, action, art direction/music, humor, and the ubiquitous moral message.

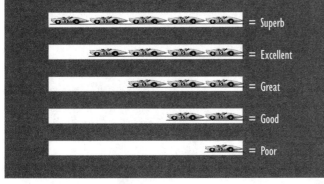

= Superb

= Excellent

= Great

= Good

= Poor

Episode 1: "The Great Plan (Part 1)"

You are watching the most advanced design and one of the fastest racing cars in the world. It's called the Mach 5. Watch it really go.

— SPEED RACER

After winning a practice race, Speed Racer is offered a position on a team set to race in the Grand Prix. The team is owned by the company who employs his father, Pops Racer, a top engineer. However, Speed declines because Pops doesn't want him to become a pro. Meanwhile, Pops quits when his plans to improve the Mach 5 are rejected.

While Pops and Speed are driving home, a gang of motorcycle racers steals their plans. Trixie,

Ace Ducey

in her helicopter, runs the gang off the road and the plans are recovered. Back at the cyclist headquarters, bad guy Ace Ducey shows up and offers to get the plans for "5,000 clams." He confronts Pops but leaves empty-handed — Pops has hidden the designs on the Mach 5's windshield using invisible ink.

Deciding to sell the Mach 5 so Pops can rebuild the engine, Speed visits Sparky, who suggests that Speed enter the Sword Mountain Race for a $5,000 prize. While Speed takes the Mach 5 out for a road test, "dirty driver" Duggery rams the car, causing it to blow a tire. In the garage, the car is repaired and is outfitted with Pops' windshield containing the hidden designs.

The race begins. Ace and his gang of drivers go after the Mach 5. Speed figures out where the plans are hidden. To avoid getting his tires shredded by Ace's gang, he hits the auto jack button. The Mach 5 is propelled over the guard rail.

Episode 2: "The Great Plan (Part 2)"

Speed resumes the Sword Mountain Race, neck and neck with Duggery. Ace and his gang approach from the opposite direction. Speed swerves off the road and uses his rotary saws to cut a path through the overgrown terrain. Trixie creates a temporary distraction, bombing the gang with smoke flares from her plane. At a crossroad, Duggery decides to take a "shortcut." Speed knows that the road leads to a dangerous volcano and sets out to rescue him.

Meanwhile, Ace and his gang fire at Trixie. The plane plummets but Trixie escapes. At the edge of the volcano, Duggery is thrown from his car, and left dangling from a rock. Speed also ends up on a rock shelf after trying to rescue his competitor. They manage to reach safety but find that the Mach 5 is surrounded by the gang, with Trixie taken hostage.

Spritle and Chim Chim, who have hidden in the Mach 5's trunk, throw rocks at the gang while Speed, Duggery, and Trixie fight them off. Ace takes off in the Mach 5. Speed follows in hot pursuit in Ace's race car — "What kind of cheap car is this?" Speed catches up to him, jumps into the Mach 5, and wrestles the pistol out of Ace's hand. With his foot, Ace accidentally hits the auto jack button, which propels him out of the car. Speed slams on the brakes. The car comes to a halt. Ace reappears. Speed hurls his helmet at the Mach 5, shattering its windshield. He kicks Ace off the cliff. Returning to the race, Speed passes Duggery and wins.

Episode 3: "Challenge of the Masked Racer (Part 1)"

He's raced against some of the top racers in the world and has beaten them just like that. Nobody's ever seen them, and they don't know who he is or where he's from.

— SPEED RACER,
describing the Masked Racer

Speed and Trixie drive to the shipyard where the Masked Racer's car is being unloaded for the upcoming Trans Country Race. Trixie hints to Speed that he should enter the race. He hesitantly agrees.

At the Racer homestead, while watching TV, Pops learns that Speed has entered the race. He "blows a gasket" and reminisces about the loss of his oldest son, Rex, who joined a race without his permission. At the brink of victory, Rex crashed the car Pops had built. Although Rex was uninjured, Pops refused to let him drive again, citing Rex's lack of experience. Consequently, Rex vowed never to return home.

Meanwhile, the Alpha Team is holding a secret conference to plot a way to win the race. Mr. Wiley tells Mr. Fixer and Alpha Team driver Zoomer Slick to "pull the dirty trick first."

Determined to beat the Masked Racer, Speed sneaks out in the middle of the night and goes to the track. Despite heavy rains he is not deterred. The Masked Racer warns him to stay out of the race. Speed answers that he wants to beat him and they "race blindly into the night." Speed crashes when an unknown person cuts a rope, causing a cascade of logs to block the track. He tumbles out of his car, losing consciousness.

POPS: "I don't want to find you behind the wheel of a car again."
REX: "Then I'll have to become a champion without you, so I'm leaving home. Good-bye, Pops."

Episode 4: "Challenge of the Masked Racer (Part 2)"

The Masked Racer takes Speed to his house. He is really Speed's older brother, Rex Racer. Speed awakens. A quick look around the room finds the Masked Racer in the shower and his mask on the chair. Speed tries on the mask and is knocked unconscious by an intruder. Outside the house, Trixie arrives and sees "the Masked Racer" seated between two men. She asks if they've seen Speed. They drive away with Spritle and Chim Chim hiding in the trunk.

At Wiley's mansion, Speed's mask is removed. Fixer walks in with Spritle and Chim Chim as prisoners; Chim Chim escapes and finds Trixie. Speed and Spritle are tied up. Ultimately, the Masked Racer rescues them.

On race day, the Racers watch the event on television. At the track, Spritle overhears Mr. Fixer give his thugs the order to fill the Masked Racer's radiator with gasoline. Spritle and Chim Chim switch the drums so that an Alpha Team member's car explodes. The Masked Racer's car blows a tire, but he continues on three wheels. However, after someone in the stands shines a mirror in his face, he spins out of control. With one lap to go before the finish line, Speed goes back to help the Masked Racer. He tells Speed to continue with the race. Speed wins and Pops lets Speed become a professional driver.

Episode 5: "The Secret Engine (Part 1)"

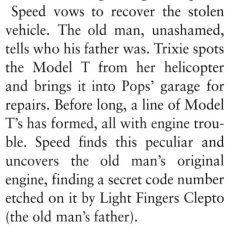

He was bad. A first-class crook, but I loved him because he'd been such a good father.

— LIGHT FINGERS CLEPTO JR.

Speed, Spritle, and Chim Chim take the Mach 5 out for a test drive. The radio announces that Tongue Blaggard has escaped from prison. The Racers meet a girl and her grandfather whose Model T has broken down on the road. Speed offers to help, but the old man declines.

Later, the Racers find the broken down Model T again. This time, the old man accepts Speed's help. While the Racers dine with the old man, the granddaughter, and his adopted children, Blaggard steals the Model T, hoping that it is the one that once belonged to the crook Light Fingers Clepto.

Speed vows to recover the stolen vehicle. The old man, unashamed, tells who his father was. Trixie spots the Model T from her helicopter and brings it into Pops' garage for repairs. Before long, a line of Model T's has formed, all with engine trouble. Speed finds this peculiar and uncovers the old man's original engine, finding a secret code number etched on it by Light Fingers Clepto (the old man's father).

Light Fingers Clepto Jr.

At his hideout, Blaggard reminisces about his encounter with the inmate who told him of the Model T's secret engine number leading to "the loot." Deciding to bait Blaggard, Speed adorns the Mach 5 with a flag bearing the engine's secret code. Blaggard's men follow while a cargo helicopter flies overhead. The thugs open fire on Speed and the old man. Suddenly, Racer X arrives ready to defend his brother, but he winds up on the edge of a cliff. The helicopter lowers a ramp unloading a squad of weapon-carrying motorcyclists.

Episode 6: "The Secret Engine (Part 2)"

Speed avoids colliding with Tongue Blaggard's squad of motorcyclists. But he is knocked out by Tiny, Blaggard's sumo bodyguard. To save Mr. Clepto from Tiny's death-grip, Speed tells Blaggard the location of what we learn is $1 billion in gold. Speed telephones Pops and leaves Trixie a message: forget about the $650 ring — a signal for help.

Guarded by Blaggard's men, Speed, in his Mach 5, heads to Misty Valley, the location of the hidden treasure. They overnight in a lodge and Speed radios for help. However, Blaggard stops him and accidentally sends the homing robot home.

Meanwhile, at the Racers, Pops is awakened by Trixie, who says she was "stood up" by Speed.

Sprile blames the homing robot for waking him. Alarmed, Trixie rushes off to find Speed.

The next morning, one of Blaggard's thugs enters the lodge with Lana, a Misty Valley native (Trixie in disguise). On the road, "Lana" and Speed escape and proceed to a village where Pops waits. Blaggard gets there first. Once again, they all continue to Misty Valley.

At the secret site, the loot is recovered. Blaggard orders his men to shoot everyone. But Spritle and Chim Chim (who have hidden aboard Trixie's helicopter), along with a gang of monkeys, hail the bad guys with stones. Speed fights off the thugs. Out of nowhere, Racer X saves them. Refusing to give up, Blag-

Tongue Blaggard

Inspector Detector congratulates Speed.

gard runs to his car with the loot. Speed follows. He directs the homing robot to knock the loot out of Blaggard's hand. The bills spill out and disintegrate into dust. Inspector Detector arrives and rewards Speed with $100,000. Speed donates the money to Mr. Clepto to start a home for orphaned children.

Episode 7: "The Race against the Mammoth Car (Part 1)"

The Car's equipped with everything anyone can imagine.
— INSPECTOR DETECTOR

Trixie wins the position of Speed's assistant in the No Limit World Race. Before the race begins, Inspector Detector and his officials search each entry looking for $50 million in stolen gold bars. The Mammoth Car enters the track. Cruncher Block gives the Inspector a tour, yielding no trace of the gold.

The race begins. The Mammoth Car forces everyone off the road. Speed is suspicious. To discover the Mammoth Car's secret, he equips the homing robot with X-ray film able to penetrate metal. Unfortunately, it's shot down and returns broken. The Mammoth Car catches up to Speed and forces the Mach 5 off the road. A ramp is lowered and a squad of motorcyclists descends onto the track. Racer X appears and spritzes oil on the road, causing the cyclists to crash.

Meanwhile, at the airport, Sprite and Chim Chim stow away aboard Cruncher Block's plane.

"Start your engines! The Gorgeous Miss Racing Car will lower the flag for the start of the 500-mile No Limit World Race."

Mammoth Car driver

Back on the track, the Mach 5 and the Mammoth Car collide and both veer off the road toward a forest. While Speed uses his rotary saws to cut

45

down the trees, the power of the Mammoth Car mows its own path. Speed backtracks and tries to slash the Car's tires. The Mammoth Car avoids this. Guns emerge from its sides. Speed raises his deflector shield to block the shower of bullets. Finally, Speed escapes through a gap and plunges into a lake.

Episode 8: "The Race against the Mammoth Car (Part 2)"

Satisfied that the Mach 5 is forever submerged in Lake Icy Chill, the Mammoth Car drivers resume the race. Through his telescanner, Speed sees them leave as he reaches soil. Trixie sends a message in the homing robot to Inspector Detector. The stolen gold is aboard the Mammoth Car. From his plane, Cruncher Block sees the Mach 5 on the road. At the refueling station, Speed and Trixie are fired at.

Escaping into a mining tunnel, they jump on top of a speeding trolley car, which crashes.

Meanwhile, at the refueling station, Sprite and Chim Chim sneak out of Cruncher's plane. They, too, escape into the tunnel, which turns out to be Cruncher's headquarters. There, Speed and Trixie are tied to a trolley loaded with three tons of dynamite. Ultimately, Racer X arrives and saves them.

At the next checkpoint, the Inspector searches the Mammoth Car. Again, he finds nothing. Speed reaches the checkpoint; Sprite and Chim Chim slip out to hide in the Mammoth Car. The Mach 5 and the Mammoth Car approach the finish line and tie for first place, but they continue at breakneck speed toward a shipyard. Sprite and Chim Chim knock out the Car's driver. Speed jumps in and then flees with his brother and chimp just as the Car collides with an oil tank, causing it to melt into a pool of molten gold.

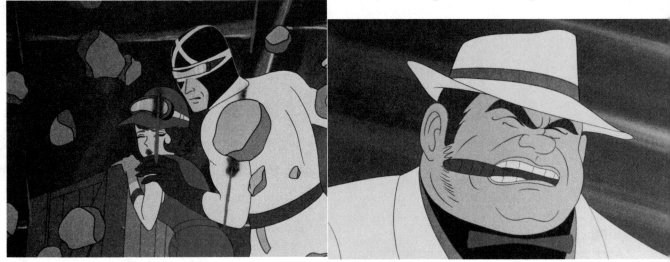

Racer X saves the day!   *Cruncher Block*

Episode 9: "The Most Dangerous Race (Part 1)"

Every time a driver tries to make it, some more of the earth caves in. And, it's going to be worse when we try to make the jump. But, as a professional racer, I've got to meet the challenge.

— SPEED RACER

"Members of the Car Acrobatic Team, tomorrow the Great Alpine Race begins — a race which we must not lose. Now, let us gather our strength from the violence of the elements."

— CAPTAIN TERROR

At the racetrack, the Stunt Car Spectacular promises "action and thrills." Two contestants attempt to scale a ramp and clear a stack of cars, but fail. Daredevil driver (and member of the Car Acrobatic Team) Snake Oiler urges Speed to try. Speed, instead, challenges Snake to the upcoming Big Alpine Race.

Later, Speed and Pops head toward a difficult section of the course where each driver must leap over a deep cavern without plunging into the river 1,000 feet below. At the site, the Car Acrobatic Team demonstrates their remarkable ability, twirling in the air over the cavern. Before Speed's attempt, Racer X offers advice.

At Pops' garage, Pops wishes he knew the secret behind the abilities of the Car Acrobatic automobiles. Sprite and Chim Chim overhear this and sneak away at night to spy on the team. Sprite returns with photographs detailing the special devices that make the cars fly. Before long, the Mach 5 is outfitted with wings. Pops passes out from exhaustion. Trixie takes him to the hospital. Speed heads to the track, noticing a problem with the brakes along the way.

Episode 10: "The Most Dangerous Race (Part 2)"

Speed is competing in the Big Alpine Race. At a checkpoint, an official warns Speed of impending bad weather. Meanwhile, fearful that the Mach 5's brakes will fail, Sparky, Sprite, and Chim Chim set out to reach Speed with new brakes. Something "goes wrong" with Sparky's car. Luckily, Trixie rescues them in her helicopter. On an icy road, Speed tries to pull ahead of the Car Acrobatic Team. The team thwarts Speed's attempt by knocking down icicles. Rounding an icy curve, the Mach 5's brakes fail. The car spins out of control and slides down the mountainside. Speed radios Trixie for help.

The next morning, Speed catches up to Snake Oiler whose car, along with others, is stopped at the most treacherous part of the course. Because of heavy rains, any car attempting to jump over the cavern would be sure to cause a landslide. The drivers decide to draw lots. Speed jumps and joins the wreckage below.

Episode 11: "The Most Dangerous Race (Part 3)"

It is the second day of the Big Alpine Race and no one has been able to cross the chasm except for Racer X. In a nearby lodge, Trixie, Sparky, Sprite, and Chim Chim await the passage of the storm. Two drivers deliver the news of what happened at the pass. Trixie and the gang leave in her helicopter to rescue Speed.

The next morning, Speed regains consciousness, discovering that he is unable to see. Somehow, he finds the Mach 5 and starts its engine. Snake Oiler cruises by "on his way to victory." Using his acute sense of hearing, Speed follows the sound of Racer X's car, which leads him back onto the racecourse. However, the Mach 5's wheels get stuck and Racer X leaves him behind. What goes around, comes around: Racer X crashes, his legs apparently broken. Speed finds him and, together

as a team in the Mach 5, they plan to overtake Snake and win the race. (Secretly, only we know that Racer X's legs are "perfectly all right," but it's his way of helping his brother.)

Speed and Racer X catch up to Snake. Speed's eyesight returns, and he sees that Snake's car is leaking oil. Speed warns his opponent, but Snake drives ahead. His car explodes. Speed wins the race. Snake vows vengeance. Racer X silently slips away.

Episode 12: "Race for Revenge (Part 1)

Lilly, have you forgotten that years ago the Melange was wrecked by a car owned by the Three Roses Club? He was knocked off the racecourse by men who cared more for winning than they did for a man's life.

— SLASH MARKER JR.

While out on a practice race, Speed is almost run off the track by a mysterious black car. Later that night, the black car gains on an automobile whose driver recognizes it as the X3. Before causing the auto to crash, the black car broadcasts, "Melange still races." A second car is also caused to crash.

The next day, Inspector Detector asks for Speed's help. While Sprite and Chim Chim hide in the Mach 5's trunk with a tape recorder, a chase ensues, but the X3 outdistances Speed. Sprite produces a tape recording of the X3's message. Pops

"The man who is behind that wheel is a reckless driver. I think that car means bad luck. I hope it's not for me."

— *Speed*

On race day, the Melange lines up beside the Three Roses Club cars. Slash Jr. vows to take Speed out first. During the race, Speed discovers Lilly is the driver of the Melange.

Episode 13: "Race for Revenge (Part 2)"

With Lilly passed out at the wheel, Speed realizes that the Melange is being driven by Slash Jr. via remote control. Unable to overtake it, Speed pulls over and discovers that Trixie has stowed away. Up ahead, the Melange approaches the Three Roses Club cars. Trixie sends a message in the homing robot that car number 3 is really the X3 Melange. Meanwhile, the Melange causes two of the Club cars to crash. Speed takes a shortcut over the mountain. He intersects the remaining Club car and the Melange car. Slash Jr. follows overhead, shooting at Speed. The sound of the gunfire, coupled with the thunder of the helicopter, causes an avalanche. Speed and Trixie climb to safety.

explains that the recent victims were the coaches of the Three Roses Club race team, the expected victors of the Danger Pass Race. However, they were worried they might be beaten by Slash Marker driving car number X3, the Melange. Mysteriously, the Melange crashed. Pops recalls that Slash had two children — Slash Jr. and Lilly.

The Inspector, Speed, and Trixie pay the siblings a visit and learn that they know nothing. Later, Lilly tells her brother that she won't lie for him again. Slash Jr. takes her to a secret workshop where he has rebuilt the Melange X3 car. Because he is crippled, he asks Lilly to drive in the upcoming Danger Pass Race.

Meanwhile, Inspector Detector, Pops, and a convoy of police officials head out to capture Slash Jr. Speed catches up to the driverless Melange. While Trixie takes over the Mach 5's steering wheel, Speed jumps into the Melange. Unfortunately, Speed is too late, and the Melange collides with the third Club car. Both cars plunge into the valley below. Inspector Detector and the gang arrive to watch Slash Jr.'s helicopter crash. Speed swims to safety in a river near the crash site.

52 Laps around the Track

Episode 14: "The Desperate Desert Race (Part 1)"

🏎️🏎️🏎️

I'll prove it. I don't have to do things like that to win races. I can win them fair and square. I've got to convince Kim I didn't blow up his car.

— SPEED RACER

Speed, along with Trixie, Sparky, and the Mach 5 are on their way to Sandoland to compete in the Desert Race. Kim Jugger tells Speed that "he doesn't have a chance of winning." He orders the workmen to load his car, the Black Tiger, first. Sprite and Chim Chim disguise themselves and board the plane. After frightening the stewardess, they escape into the cargo area. A one-eyed man enters and the two youngsters see him plant a time bomb in Kim's race car.

Upon landing, the Black Tiger explodes. Kim

"There's a scorpion on you. Don't move!"
— KIM JUGGER to Speed

accuses Speed of ordering his brother to sabotage his car. Speed denies the accusation and a fight ensues. At the hotel, Sprite tells Speed what happened in the airplane. Determined to prove his innocence, Speed and Trixie head out to Flathill Country, Kim's homeland. After surviving a sandstorm, the Mach 5 is surrounded by rebel soldiers. Unfortunately, the Mach 5 crashes when it autojacks over a sand dune. The rebels take Speed and company to a desert fortress where Kim lives with his father, the General of the Flathill Army. Sprite identifies the one-eyed man, Ali Ben Schemer, as the culprit. Schemer orders the soldiers to lock Speed in jail and to burn the Mach 5.

Episode 15: "The Desperate Desert Race (Part 2)"

While the Flathill Army soldiers set the Mach 5 aflame, Speed attacks one of the rebels. The General announces that he ordered Ali Ben Schemer, his cousin, to blow up his son's race car because they need his help in the revolution. When Kim notes that his special brakes can never be repaired, Schemer suggests that Kim and Speed race without brakes. The next morning, Schemer gives them a sack lunch and the race begins. He then takes Trixie, Sprite, and the General prisoner. Chim Chim rescues Sprite and they escape on a camel. Meanwhile, as the Black Tiger and the Mach 5 race through the desert, the sack "lunches" open, revealing deadly scorpions. Kim realizes what Schemer is up to. The scorpions are smashed; the race resumes.

Later, Sprite and Chim Chim are rescued by

members of the Flathill Government Army, who are after the rebels. Back on the racecourse, the Black Tiger is devoured by quicksand. Kim, Speed, and the Mach 5 almost meet the same fate. But they, too, are rescued by the Government Army. All head back to the fortress. Trixie is rescued just before the fortress explodes.

Episode 16: "The Fire Race (Part 1)"

I've risked my life to save your treasure. Now, you gentlemen must come to some agreement. Compromise. Open your borders to the world some of the time.

— RACER X

At a meeting of the League of Countries, the representative from Kapecapek announces his government's decision to close its borders to the outside world. An official proposes that if Kapecapek's race car driver, named Kabala, beats Speed Racer, then its borders can remain closed. At the racetrack, Speed receives an invitation to the Fire Festival Race. Speed finds this peculiar because Kapecapek doesn't have a racetrack and Kabala has been missing for a long time. Nevertheless, Speed and company arrive in Kapecapek. They spot Racer X, who was also invited.

That night Chief Zuma lets it be known that "the winner of the race will be bridegroom" to his

granddaughter, Princess Sibana. He points out Speed as the probable winner. But when a jealous Trixie makes it clear that Speed is taken, another driver, Mr. Kadar, steps forward with his offer of matrimony.

Later, Mr. Kadar captures the Princess and demands to know where the country's treasure is hidden. Speed comes to her rescue. The next day, the racers and their cars are carried by raft to a secret entrance in a volcanic mountain. The racers drive through a tunnel to an ancient city with bejeweled statues. The race is set to begin once the volcano erupts. An official announces that the cars will drive through 800 miles of volcanic tunnel. Whoever reaches the exit before the split in the mountain closes will win. Amid falling debris, an unsteady terrain, and the threat of impending molten lava, the drivers line up. Kabala shows up and the race begins.

Episode 17: "The Fire Race (Part 2)"

"In the volcanic mountains of Kapecapek, Speed is competing in the most unusual race of his life." Kadar and his men find diamonds encrusted in the mountain wall. A creeping vine grabs his men (who escape), while Kadar holds Kabala

"I'm racing to win, that's all. And I'm going to do it. I'll see you at the finish line, Racer X."   — SPEED RACER

at gunpoint. Speed throws a knife knocking the gun out of Kadar's hand. A fight ensues and Kabala's mask falls off, revealing Racer X. Racer X is about to give Speed an explanation when the ground caves in. Kadar and his thugs leave with the Kapecapekian treasure.

Speed and Racer X find a way out. Racer X tells Speed that the real Kabala taught him "tricks on how to race on tortured roads and broken trails." Once Racer X turned professional, he had a race with his mentor, who, unfortunately, fell victim to a landslide. To return Kabala's kindness, Racer X disguised himself as Kabala to protect the Kapecapekian treasure.

Kadar and his men succumb to the lava flow. Speed, followed by Racer X, exits the mountain just as it erupts and seals the split. Although Speed won the race, the Chief won't concede. Speed points out that Kabala is really Racer X, who suggests that Kapecapek keep its borders open "some of the time."

Episode 18: "The Girl Daredevil (Part 1)"

Brotch is a very clever man. He's committed robberies all over the country. The police haven't caught him, so maybe we can find out where his hideout is and report it to the police.

— SPEED RACER

At the base of a tall building, Speed

and company watch Twinkle Banks, star of the Universal Circus, dive off the top. Then, at the circus, they watch Twinkle drive a race car and perform daredevil stunts. She worries about maintaining the car's momentum and faints. Speed rescues Twinkle. While the girl daredevil rests in bed, a clown (her father) tells Speed that because of a money shortage, he's having difficulty keeping the track in good repair. Speed makes a donation. Later, Speed and Trixie learn on the radio that Twinkle will drive a car, balanced on two ropes, over Niagara Falls. Because of the strong winds Speed and Trixie try to stop Twinkle.

Meanwhile, Cornpone Brush, who financed the stunt, tells the clown that Twinkle will perform regardless of the hazardous weather. When Speed and Trixie arrive, Twinkle is already making her way across the Falls. Away from the crowd, Brush reads an old map. It identifies a secret cave in back of the Falls that leads to treasure. His thugs lower a gigantic pipeline into the Falls and Brush drives into it to discover the cave's entrance.

Back at the stunt show, the wind causes Twinkle's car to plunge into the Falls, leaving her hanging onto one of the ropes. Speed drives the Mach 5 on two wheels down the remaining rope to rescue Twinkle. He grabs her. The rope snaps and

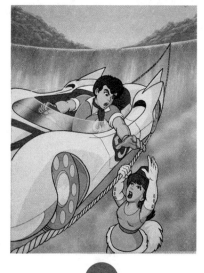

Adjusted to drive on ropes, the Mach 5 and Speed set out to rescue Twinkle Banks.

they plunge into the Falls. Attempting to drive along the bottom, Speed gets caught in a series of whirlpools. With little oxygen left in the cockpit, Speed and Twinkle pass out.

Episode 19: "The Girl Daredevil (Part 2)"

Speed and Twinkle awake back into consciousness. They enter the cave behind the Falls. Cornpone Brotch (identified as Cornpone *Brush* in the previous episode) and his thugs arrive with the treasure. Speed fights off the thugs, while Brotch escapes in the Mach 5.

Using her experience as an escape artist, Twinkle frees herself and Speed from the ropes that bind them. Trixie, in her helicopter, along with Spritle and Chim Chim, spots Brotch in the Mach 5. Speed and Twinkle exit the cave; Trixie picks them up. Brotch enters his secret hideout located in Mount Rushmore. Later that night, Speed and the gang find the secret entrance.

Inside the mountain, Speed and company find collections of stolen art and cars, including the Mach 5. Brotch surrounds them with ferocious black panthers. While Speed fights the cats, Twinkle jumps to safety, hanging from a chandelier. Meanwhile, Trixie races in the Mach 5 to save her friends. Brotch locks them all in the room. Sleeping gas seeps through vents in the wall and the panthers pass out. Speed and company are protected by the Mach 5's deflector shield. With a handkerchief over his face, Speed jumps out of his car and opens the door. Spritle and Chim Chim feed the panthers candy; the cats attack the thugs. Finally, Speed, Trixie, and Twinkle escape. They enter a room where a lion sits in a cage, connected to another with Twinkle's father inside. Brotch tells them to step back or he'll let the lion into the clown's cage. Twinkle reminds her father that he used to be the best animal trainer in the world. The clown stares down the lion. Riding atop the panthers, Spritle and Chim Chim come to the rescue.

Later, at Niagara Falls, Twinkle performs her trick again. This time, the clown accompanies her in the vehicle. The clown is Speed in disguise.

Episode 20: "The Fastest Car on Earth (Part 1)"

I've never driven so fast in my life. This speed is taking me into another dimension. It's fantastic!

— Speed Racer

"Huh? The GRX? This is that famous engine. I'm not dreaming. I'm really looking right at the GRX!"

At midnight in a cemetery, the GRX race car engine is unearthed. The following day Spritle and Chim Chim are trapped inside a truck. It takes them to Oriana Flub's house, where Chim Chim is tied to a motorized go-cart. When the chimp comes to a stop, one of Oriana's men sprays a "formula" at him. As he takes off again, Oriana announces that "they'll win the Grand Prix of the Orient."

At the track, a new race car comes on the scene. Pops recognizes the sound of its engine. High in the stands, Oriana and her right-hand man, Omar, watch while a thug sprays the driver of the mysterious car with the formula. At Oriana's house, Pops accuses her of stealing the engine "out of the tomb of Bent Cranium," the engine's inventor. Pops adds that five test drivers and Cranium died because of the GRX. Oriana knocks him out with "sleeper gas."

Meanwhile, Speed in the Mach 5, along with Trixie and Sparky, follows a flatbed truck carrying the GRX race car. Inside the truck's cab, the man on the passenger side is desperate for water. After he gulps several mouthfuls, he becomes delusional and begs the driver to slow down. The truck pulls into Oriana's garage. Spritle and Chim Chim, who have been lurking in the bushes, spot Speed on the truck. In another room, Pops is being beaten.

In the garage, Speed discovers the famous GRX engine. A man named Curly appears. A fight ensues. Meanwhile, Spritle and Chim Chim rescue Pops, who's tied to a chair. Speed knocks out Curly. As if hypnotized by the car, Speed gets inside to "try it just once." The high speed takes Speed into another dimension and he passes out.

Episode 21: "The Fastest Car on Earth (Part 2)"

Speed has passed out behind the wheel of the GRX. Eventually, the car comes to a halt at the edge of an aqueduct. Spritle and Chim Chim drag Speed out of the race car. One of Oriana's thugs gets in the GRX and drives away.

At the Racer homestead Pops sets out to "cure" Speed of his delusions. Later at the racetrack, the final trials for the Oriental Grand Prix are about to begin. Oriana's thug squirts the formula at Louis Towcar so that he can "stand the speed of the GRX." Further, he warns the driver that if he drinks water while he is driving, "you'll get so scared, you'll lose control of the car and smash into smithereens."

The race begins. Towcar tries to quench his insatiable thirst. A chemical reaction takes effect and Towcar passes out. Speed autojacks over the GRX, which blows up. Later, in her helicopter, Oriana asks Speed to drive the GRX in the upcoming race.

Speed gets into the repaired GRX race car. The thug gives him the formula. He takes off. Upon spotting Speed in the GRX, Trixie lands her helicopter in Speed's path. Pops rushes over to Speed. At home, Pops once again tries to deprogram his son. Dr. Skuller reports to Pops that his son has inhaled V gas.

On race day, Speed is "scared and can't help it." Pops tells him to be a man. Curly, driving the GRX, vows to win. The race begins. Speed races ahead, Pops' advice ringing in his ears. Curly goes into the pit and runs for water. As he resumes the race, he becomes delusional. The GRX spins out of control, bursting into flames. Speed pulls into the lead and wins the race. We then learn that Curly was the son of the GRX's inventor

Episode 22: "The Mach 5 vs. the Mach 5 (Part 1)"

If that were an ordinary car I can catch up to it, but I can't when it's another Mach 5.

— SPEED RACER

Late one night, Professor Power, inventor of the Mizmo Ray, leaves the Secret National Science Institute. Shortly thereafter, the Mach 5 roars toward the Institute and autojacks over its gate. Despite alarms and several rounds of ammunition, the mysterious driver escapes unscathed. The next morning on TV, a reporter broadcasts the news of a theft at the Institute.

Inspector Detector asks Speed to come down to his office. At Police Headquarters, the security guards identify the Mach 5. Speed says that he met a girl named Lorena and that her father, Dr. Nightcall, invited him in for dinner. However, Speed's alibi is in doubt when Lorena and her father deny meeting him. Nightcall has a teleconference with his boss, Mr. Cumulous. He is ordered to build a copy of the Mach 5. Together, Nightcall and Cumulous conspire to rule the world.

At the Racer homestead, a disgruntled Pops can't figure out how the Mach 5 could have been at the scene of the crime. In exchange for cake, Spritle tells Trixie what happened while he and Chim Chim hid in Speed's car. From outside the Nightcall house, they saw Speed fall asleep. After Lorena left the room, the doctor left in the Mach 5.

Trixie relays Spritle's story to Inspector Detector, who presents Dr. Nightcall with a search warrant. Nightcall and Lorena escape. Speed and Trixie follow in the Mach 5. On a mountain road, they meet an identical Mach 5 driven by Cumulous. Cumulous tells the pair that his Mach 5 is equipped with a Mizmo Ray gun. Cumulous points it at Speed and Trixie.

Episode 23: "The Mach 5 vs. the Mach 5 (Part 2)"

"This proves they're guilty. Use the Mach 5 and try to catch them." — INSPECTOR DETECTOR TO SPEED

Speed guns his engine and autojacks over the Mizmo Ray beam. The Mach 5 copy blasts off into the air. Meanwhile, in the police helicopter, Inspector Detector, Spritle, and Chim Chim spot the two cars. The Mach 5 copy dives into the ocean. Cumulous reaches his headquarters, the doors closing behind him. The real Mach 5 slams into the door. Inspector Detector sends a fleet of patrol boats to search for Speed. Spritle and Chim Chim, dressed in scuba suits, fall overboard to search for Speed and Trixie.

Back at the underwater base, Lorena enters and apologizes to Speed. Cumulous discloses his "big plan." He explains that in thirty minutes missiles will destroy all military bases and force every country to surrender to him. Lorena is shocked. Grabbing a gun from his jacket, she holds Cumulous and his men at gunpoint. But Cumulous shoots her. Speed struggles with Cumulous's thugs.

Extra baggage!

Sprtile and Chim Chim appear and clobber the countdown operator of the missile blastoff. Speed, Trixie, and Cumulous witness this on a TV monitor. Cumulous hurries to the Mach 5. Speed follows. Trixie radios the Inspector. As Cumulous heads toward the city, stowaway Spritle puts his hands in front of Cumulous's eyes while Chim Chim pounds on his head. Speed catches up to the car. Trixie takes the wheel as Speed jumps into the Mach 5 copy. He pushes Cumulous out of the car. Dr. Nightcall vows to convert the base and dedicate it to Lorena.

Episode 24: "The Royal Racer (Part 1)"

I assure you, your royal, imperial, majestic, highness, the car's in tip-top condition. It's fit for a king to drive, even a future king.

— POPS RACER

The King of Saccarin has asked Pops to build a mini race car for the Baby Grand Prix to be held in celebration of the coronation of Prince Jam. Spritle pleads with his father to build him a car for the race. Pops explains that he is too young. Disappointed, Spritle storms out in a huff.

In Saccarin, the Mach 5 pulls a flatbed with the Prince's car on top. A piece of luggage falls off; Spritle and Chim Chim spill out. At the palace, the King proclaims the car "a masterpiece of automotive art." A dopey-looking Prince watches. The King explains that he's Prince Sugarin, a cousin.

Spritle and his pet stumble upon a parade featuring Prince Jam, who looks a great deal like Spritle.

From the top of a building, three black-clad individuals (resembling bats) appear and try to kidnap Prince Jam. Fortunately, the Prince manages to get away. Inside a temple, the two look-alike boys collide. The bat boys and Speed arrive. Speed fights them off. The palace soldiers arrive. Mistaking Spritle for the Prince, they whisk him off to the palace. Speed leaves with "Spritle" under his arm.

Later that night, a man named Omar conspires with Minister Offendem to put Prince Sugarin on the throne in order to gain control of Saccarin. At the palace, Spritle decides to keep up the charade. The royal "Spritle" is punished and locked up in the Racers' hotel room closet. Eventually, he escapes.

On the track, the mini race cars line up. The bat boys surround the royal racing car, causing it to jump off the track. The car is stranded on a bridge. The bat boys cut the bridge's suspension cables. As Speed arrives, the bridge collapses. Both cars plummet into the jungle below.

Episode 25: "The Royal Racer (Part 2)"

The mini race car and the Mach 5 "tumble into the jungle," where "the royal racer" explodes. Offendem convinces the King that Pops Racer is to blame. Also, Offendem urges him to agree that Prince Sugarin should ascend the throne.

Back in the jungle, Speed, Spritle, and Chim Chim set out in the Mach 5 to rescue the real Prince (who Speed believes is still in the hotel's closet). Meanwhile, Prince Jam begs for food in the bazaar. His claims of being the Prince of Saccarin are met with laughter. In his hotel room, Speed encounters the bat boys. They attack, but Speed manages to alert Sprite.

Two of the bat boys escape with Speed in the Mach 5. The other is held hostage by Spritle and all the other drivers. Breaking into two groups, one takes Spritle disguised as Prince Jam to the palace. The other group takes the bat boy to get the real Prince Jam. Just as Prince Sugarin is being crowned, "Prince Jam" appears and "reunites" with the King. He points to Offendem as the culprit. Meanwhile, Chim Chim, who has disguised himself in a bat boy costume, rescues Speed and the real Prince. The second group of drivers escorts them to the palace. Offendem walks away, defeated.

Back at the garage, Spritle pouts. Speed points out that, in fact, Spritle is eligible to compete. A race car is built. Sprite and Prince Jam tie for first place.

Episode 26: "The Car Hater"

MR. TROTTER: *All cars are weapons on wheels.*
SPEED: *When they're driven right, they're perfectly safe, sir.*

Trixie is behind the wheel of the Mach 5. A car full of bullies pulls alongside and taunts her. Fortunately, Speed's quick reflexes help to avoid a collision. The Mach 5 autojacks over the bullies' vehicle. When they realize it's the Mach 5 and "the best racer in the world," the bullies befriend Speed.

Trixie meets a young woman named Janine. She offers her a chance to drive the Mach 5. Janine tells Trixie that she wants to become a race car driver but her father won't let her. As they're driving, a man on horseback darts in front of the car and Janine slams on the brakes. The horseman turns out to be her father, Mr. Trotter, who takes a whip to the Mach 5. Speed comes to the rescue just as Trotter is about to whip his daughter. Trotter confesses that he lost his son in a car accident.

Later, Trotter reads a newspaper, disgusted by the number of car accidents. He reiterates to Janine how he doesn't want her around cars. However, after reading an article about the opening of a

new racetrack, she leaves. Trotter spots the article and goes after her on his horse. In an attempt to prove how dangerous cars are, Trotter hires three thugs to sabotage automobiles all over the city.

"Listen, stop driving cars. They're much too dangerous."
— MR. TROTTER

Speed and Janine Trotter

That night, Trotter demands to know where Janine is. Speed tells him she and Trixie are out test driving a new car. A thug informs them he has "fixed" the brakes on that car. Speed sets out to rescue the girls. Trixie is uninjured. He takes Janine to the hospital. Upon Trotter's release from prison, father and daughter reunite. Pops presents Trotter with a sports car. Janine is allowed to become a race car driver.

Episode 27: "The Race against Time (Part 1)"

I'll try to win the next race, Trixie. But right now, I've got something more important to do. Even though I couldn't help Dr. Bone when he was alive, maybe I can still help him.

— SPEED RACER

While competing in the Sahara Race, Speed rescues an old man who's running away from a low-flying airplane. The man identifies himself as Dr. Digger O. Bone, archaeologist. With his last breath, Bone asks Speed to find his daughter, Calcia, who with his assistant, Splint Femur, have discovered Cleopatra's tomb. He scrawls four letters in the sand and dies.

In a library, Trixie deciphers the code that will lead them to the tomb. At the tomb they are

"That's the largest cobra I've ever seen!"

— SPEED RACER

shot at, fight off guards, get trapped beneath stone debris, and wrestle a giant cobra. Then, Cleopatra orders them jailed for daring to enter her sacred palace.

Speed recognizes "Cleopatra" as Calcia. A cloaked man turns out to be Splint Femur. He vows to get rid of them. "Cleopatra" has convinced the slaves to cooperate and help dig up "her" treasure. Later, at Cleopatra's court, a packed audience watches as Speed is led into an arena to fight "the best swordsman in the country," Tetconkin. Speed wins. He is then told to bring them the statue of Isis, located on top of a distant pyramid. This he must do within two hours, before a shadow reaches the eyes of a statue in the Queen's palace. If Speed fails, Trixie, who is tied to a stake, will die.

Speed takes off in the Mach 5. Femur's soldiers follow in a jeep, firing their machine guns. Speed uses his rotary saws to counterattack, slashing the jeep's tires. As Speed reaches the pyramid, Femur orders the palace soldiers to ignite the stake holding Trixie.

Episode 28: "The Race against Time (Part 2)"

Speed is near the top of the pyramid. He is being shot at from an airplane. He throws the homing robot, attached to the climbing rope, toward the plane. The rope is wound around the propeller and the plane crashes. Speed grabs the statue of Isis. Meanwhile, Trixie is lowered into the fire. Just as the shadow reaches the eye of the palace statue, homing robot and statue arrive. "Cleopa-

59

52 Laps around the Track

tra" spares their lives but sentences Speed and Trixie to slavery. Picks in hand, hungry and tired, they recognize Spritle's voice coming from the Queen's perch atop her elephant.

Later that night, Spritle rescues them. Trixie finds Calcia and straightens her out. They all proceed to the Mach 5 only to discover the gas tank empty. Femur appears, telling "Cleopatra" that she has been misled. Once again, the group is forced into slavery, except for Speed. Femur forces him and the Mach 5 off the cliff into the Nile River below.

That same night, Spritle escapes and frees the other slaves. Femur orders his soldiers to fire at them. But suddenly, Speed, with police support, fires first. Femur refuses to surrender. Pandemonium breaks out when a giant stone statue arises. The palace starts to crumble. "Cleopatra" is hit by falling rocks. Speed runs to the Mach 5. He anchors the homing robot and rope to the statue's eye and climbs to enter the control room. He fires at the control panel, causing the stone god to collapse. Femur flees with the treasure to his airplane. Speed follows. Calcia appears in the cockpit and holds Femur at gunpoint. He forces the plane into a dive, but Speed comes to the rescue. He and Calcia parachute safely into the river.

Episode 29: "The Snake Track"

He can drive on only two wheels even with just one hand on the steering wheel. The Snake Track means nothing to a driver like that. Who is he anyway?
— SPEED RACER

At an international airport, Rock Force is met by a mysterious man and confronted by a group of thugs wanting to know if he will compete in the upcoming Super Car Race. A fight ensues. Rock clobbers them all.

In a helicopter, Speed, Trixie, Sparky, Spritle, and Chim Chim look down on

Speed and Rock Force

the curving Snake Track course. Speed is determined to win this race. Later, Speed and Trixie spend the afternoon relaxing in a meadow. A team of race cars pass by, chasing another car that tips onto two wheels. Speed sends the homing robot to the rescue. He then drives alongside Rock's car, marveling at his automatic transmission and driving skill. Quickly, Speed realizes that Rock's ability to cut sharp curves by driving on two wheels is just the technique needed to maneuver the Mach 5.

At the race, Speed tries out the technique, but his car flips over. That night, Rock discovers his race car has been sabotaged. He begs Pops to fix his car "immediately." Spritle points out a tear in Rock's jacket sleeve. Rock rips it further to reveal a right arm brace. He explains how the Rival Motor Company offered him a lot of money to lose a race. When he won, "they made sure I'd never be able to use my right arm again."

"On the other side of the city," Jack Rival orders his thugs to get rid of Rock. At the Racers' home, Rock admits he is not qualified to be a racing driver. Spritle urges Pops to invent "something" so he can have full control of his car. Speed has a better idea. He tells Rock to drive the Mach 5, convinced all Rock needs to do is "work the arm." Without automatic transmission, Rock initially refuses.

Rock wins the race. At the judging stand, the thugs show up. They point to his arm, citing it as grounds for immediate disqualification. A fight ensues. Then, after Rock realizes he has used his arm, he takes off his brace, declaring himself "completely well again." The thugs leave defeated. Speed vows to win the next race.

Episode 30: "The Man on the Lam"

LAWSON LAMSTER: You saved my life. I don't really deserve it.
SPEED RACER: I feel that everyone's life is worth saving.

On a rainy night, Lawson Lamster escapes from prison. He comes to Delicia's house. Lawson embraces the child, noticing that she is blind. He learns that her mother is away trying to earn money for Delicia's sight restoration.

The next day, Speed, Spritle, and Chim Chim arrive in the Mach 5. Lawson forces Speed into his car. Speed orders Spritle to get in the trunk, while Chim Chim stays behind to look after Delicia. Lawson promises the girl he'll return. Delicia and Chim Chim make their way to the Racers' and then to Inspector Detector. Meanwhile, a man named Stencher spies on the group. He orders his thugs to listen to the police broadcast. They must

Speed and Lawson Lamster

52 Laps around the Track

"get their hands on Lamster" and the "100,000 bucks" before the cops do.

The police spot the Mach 5 and chase after Speed. However, Stencher's men intercept. Stencher reminds Lawson how he agreed to split "the loot." The Mach 5 and a bound Speed and Lawson are loaded onto a truck.

At a dam, Lawson is released to find the loot. He is able to sneak away. Meanwhile, Spritle climbs out of the Mach 5's trunk and unties his brother. Lawson escapes in the Mach 5. Speed and Spritle go after him. Having reached a ghost town, Lawson unearths the money. Speed jumps him from a roof and they fight. Stencher and his men arrive and Speed and Lawson hide. The town is set on fire. In the midst of a shootout, Speed realizes that Lawson has disappeared. Then, from out of the flames, Lawson stumbles toward him carrying a briefcase full of money. As Stencher and Lawson battle, the briefcase opens. The bills scatter

into the flames. Speed comes to Lawson's aid. Before he dies, Lawson tells Speed to donate his eyes to Delicia.

Episode 31: "Gang of Assassins (Part 1)"

RACER X: I'm a full-fledged member of the worldwide Assassins. Are you surprised? You see, I was sick and tired of racing where I risked my neck for a few dollars and a lot of glory. I'll get more here.
SPEED : And I thought you were decent. You're rotten!

"One hundred thousand racing fans saw the race which turned out to be one of the most exciting races in history. At times, it was a dead heat as those two champion drivers, Speed Racer and Racer X, demonstrated their unexcelled driving skills. And then, Speed Racer won brilliantly."

Early morning in Japan, the Gang of Assassins breaks into an ancient castle to plant a time bomb. Later, at the Fujiyama Grand Prix, Speed wins, and Racer X vows to beat him the next time. Trixie and Speed leave to go sightseeing. When Trixie turns on the radio for news of the race, Speed gloats. In other news, they learn President Crackbrow and his ministers from the country of Aquarian have been killed by a bomb.

With many international figures visiting Japan for the Piecemeal Conference, the police have beefed up security. At Splendor Castle, the Gang of Assassins gases the security guards. Speed and Trixie investigate. The Assassins spot them and toss bombs from the roof.

The next day, Racer X meets Speed, advising him to "just forget" about the Gang of Assassins because "they're too dangerous." Later, a man named Pat Gunsel approaches Racer X with a job offer. Meanwhile, Speed, Trixie, Spritle, and Chim Chim continue their investigative sight-seeing adventure. They notice a Piecemeal Conference tour boat. Nearby, Racer X watches the boat also. An Assassin catches Racer X's attention, picking a fight. Gunsel appears, declaring that he was "just putting you to a test." Gunsel points to the boat. A dragon emerges and the boat is sucked underwater. Speed follows, leaving the others behind.

Gunsel is determined to rule the world. He advises Racer X to join his organization. Unable to find "the big monster," Speed comes back to shore. Upon seeing the Gang of Assassins, he takes off in pursuit. He enters a Japanese castle — the secret hideout of the Assassins.

Episode 32: "Gang of Assassins (Part 2)"

Inside the ancient Japanese castle, Speed meets Pat Gunsel, who vows to "get rid of him." Speed is shoved past a jail cell filled with the diplomats from the sight-seeing boat. Speed watches as the Assassins exhibit their defense and driving skills. Finally, Speed is taken to Professor Anarchy. He gives Speed the choice to "either join or die." Speed refuses. He punches Gunsel, grabbing his gun. Anarchy orders Speed to drop the gun or die. Racer X offers to "take care of the kid." He knocks Speed unconscious.

Meanwhile, Trixie, Spritle, and Chim Chim look for Speed. Chim Chim spots the airborne homing robot, which leads them to the Mach 5.

"I'm a leader of this division of assassins. You should've kept away from us, but now we gotta get rid of you."
— PAT GUNSEL

Trixie drives the Mach 5 into the lake and is swallowed up too. While Spritle and Chim Chim hide in the trunk, Trixie is thrown into the cell with Speed and the diplomats.

Professor Anarchy holds a meeting of his Assassins. He instructs them to bomb the upcoming Piecemeal Conference. The prisoners are brought in. Handing Racer X a gun, Gunsel orders him to shoot them. Racer X shoots the ropes that bind the prisoners, setting them free. Racer X holds Anarchy and Gunsel at gunpoint, demanding their assassin return. After much struggle, the diplomats escape to safety. Speed and Trixie stop the Assassins and Racer X sets a time bomb to blow up the weapons' supply room. Anarchy and Gunsel escape aboard the airborne dragon submarine. Spritle and Chim Chim, who have hidden aboard the dragon, knock out the pilot with a wrench. They parachute to safety just as the dragon spirals toward the Gang of Assassins and explodes. Speed asks Racer X if he's "some kind of secret agent." Racer X answers, "I'm only a professional racing driver and your closest competitor."

Episode 33: "The Race for Life"

Don't let him be Mayor. Listen everybody, Juan was not bitten accidentally by a snake. It was part of a plot so he could take over the village.

— Spritle

In the city of Dominico, where the South American Grand Prix is being held, several gunmen chase a young man named José, who carries a first aid box. José collapses amid Speed's victory celebration. A "beautiful señorita" named Marie runs to José's aid. He gives her a serum and dies. Marie runs off. Speed and the gunmen follow. Eventually, Speed catches up to her inside an empty bullfighter's stadium. An angry bull is let loose. Fortunately, Sparky arrives in the Mach 5 and they escape.

Marie explains that her brother, Juan, needs the serum to cure a snakebite. Meanwhile, "in the distant village of Tonado," several people surround Juan's bed. A man named Francko wants to stop Marie and let Juan die. He wants to be Mayor and possess a hidden treasure.

On the way to the village, Speed wonders why someone wouldn't want Juan to recover. As the Mach 5 goes over a bridge Francko's men have sabotaged, the bridge collapses. Yet the Mach 5 reaches soil safely. Meanwhile, in the dying Juan's room, Francko snickers. On the road, Francko's men cause a landslide. The Mach 5 is trapped. Marie recognizes the men. She and Speed distract them so Spritle can get away to deliver the serum.

At the village, an old man begs Juan to "hold on." Spritle arrives with the serum just as Francko proclaims himself Mayor. Spritle interrupts, telling the assembled crowd about Francko's scheme. Speed and Marie arrive in the Mach 5. One of Francko's men sets fire to the buildings. A gunshot rings out, which causes bulls to stampede through the village. Francko, with the treasure in tow, escapes on horseback. Speed follows. Francko and his horse fall off the edge of a cliff.

Episode 34: "The Supersonic Car"

I'm glad to hear it, Speed. I always knew you weren't the kind of guy who gives up after only one failure.

— POPS RACER

On the Saline Flats, the Supersonic Rocket Car, designed by Pops, is to be tested for the Baboom Motor Company. From the control tower, Pops watches Speed blast off into the desert terrain. But the tail breaks and the vehicle explodes. Later, in the Baboom Company's conference room, one of the board members, Dante Ferno, blames the car's failure on its driver.

At the test site, an inspector points out a broken screw and later concludes that the car was sabotaged. Nevertheless, the company vows to build another car and to replace Speed as driver. Then, as applicants line up for the test drive, two men named Tycootis and Blacket plan to "do something about" the second car.

Speed reapplies for the test job and is rehired. Tycootis orders Ferno to have Speed and Pops "taken care of." The attack is unsuccessful. The second model of the Supersonic Car is built and Speed blasts off. Again, there is sabotage. The president reminds everyone that, since he's a "qualified engineer," he will conduct this investigation himself. He discovers a questionable part and interrogates a man named Twert, who runs away. Speed tackles Twert. Blacket appears, but he won't confess.

The president, Speed, and Pops set out to build a new car. At the test site, Sprite overhears

The Supersonic Rocket Car

Ferno telling Tycootis that a bomb has been planted "on the white line." Sprite and Chim Chim stow away in the Rocket Car to relay the information to Speed. Unable to stop in time, Speed accelerates instead, beating the explosion and setting a new speed record. Inspector Detector arrives to arrest Tycootis and Ferno.

Episode 35: "Crash in the Jungle (Part 1)"

I wish I can look for the monster with you, but I only have a couple of days before the race starts.

— SPEED RACER

In two days Speed will compete in the Trans Africa Grand Prix. Having finished checking the course, Speed returns in an airplane. On the flight, he meets Professor Robert Carnivory, a biologist in search of a "monster" that lives in a nearby mountain. The co-pilot turns around and at gunpoint takes Carnivory prisoner. Identifying himself as an exile of the country Bangdabongo, he explains how the Professor (a former citizen) is needed to help liberate the country. Speed is tied to a chair.

A supersized spider seeks to entwine Speed

The pilots and Carnivory parachute to the jungle. Fortunately, Speed is able to break loose and jump out of the plane before it crashes.

Meanwhile, in Nairobi, Trixie, Spritle, and Chim Chim hear a news report about the plane crash and set out in the Mach 5 to find Speed. Back in the jungle, Speed and tribesmen start off for the fiery mountain. They battle a giant spider. Later, he sees an unusual tank.

Speed follows the tank to a lake with an island in its middle. A bridge emerges from the water; the tank drives across. As the bridge submerges, Speed tries to dash across. He doesn't reach the island in time and the water swallows him. Meanwhile, Chim Chim grabs an egg from a bird's nest. When the bird returns, it flies away with Chim Chim who is still holding on to the egg. Trixie and Spritle follow in the Mach 5.

Elsewhere, a man named General Smasher tells Professor Carnivory how they have succeeded in making animals and insects larger; now they will build an army of giant humans. Carnivory refuses to cooperate. On a TV monitor, Speed is seen swimming underwater toward the island. Back in the jungle, Spritle hollers to Chim Chim to give the bird back its egg. When the monkey does so, he is dropped into the lake. Trixie follows after him. The Mach 5 drives alongside the underwater bridge. On the island, Speed climbs a tree to find the tank. He then finds himself surrounded by monster gorillas.

Episode 36: "Crash in the Jungle (Part 2)"

Speed is forced off a cliff by a gang of monster gorillas. Smasher reunites the uncooperative Professor with an old cohort, Professor Loon. Various giant creatures are revealed. Although Carnivory respects Loon's scientific work, he still does not want to help. Then, on the TV monitor, the three men watch Trixie and Spritle drive "the amphibious car." When the Mach 5 surfaces, it is met by a fleet of the mysterious tanks. One lands on the Mach 5 and Trixie and Spritle pass out.

Captured and bound, Trixie and Spritle hang over a pool of water filled with deadly piranhas. Smasher gives Carnivory an ultimatum. Meanwhile, Speed has an emotional reunion with Chim Chim and the Mach 5. They set out to find Trixie and Spritle.

On a cliff overlooking the island's interior, Speed sees the gorillas who are caged and guarded. A fleet of tanks comes up behind him, firing their cannons. In the Mach 5, he eludes them. Then, when one of the tanks halts, Speed knocks out the driver.

Back in the laboratory, Trixie and Spritle are prepared to be made supersized. But Speed crashes through the wall in the seized tank and rescues them. The gorilla breaks out of its cage. Trixie takes the wheel of the tank. Speed jumps into his Mach 5 and causes the other tanks to crash. Meanwhile, the berserk gorilla destroys the power room. The General reforms, realizing "maybe we were wrong." Speed and company escape in the Mach 5 using the underwater bridge. The island explodes. The Professor promises to restore the creatures to their normal size. Speed and the gang head to Nairobi for the race.

Episode 37: "The Terrifying Gambler"

They say that knowledge is power. And if that's so, I already have great power. Woe be it to anyone who gets in my way.

— MR. FLASHBUCKS

Speed and Trixie are competing in the Monte Carlo Rally. On an icy mountain road, an old man driving an old-fashioned car catches up to the Mach 5 and shoots at them. Speed skids to a halt. Later, Speed and Trixie look through mug shots at the

"Yes, I'm wanted by the police in half a dozen countries. And I'm at the top of the Interpol list. I'm wanted for robbery, murder, swindling, and cheating at dominoes."
— MR. FLASHBUCKS

52 Laps around the Track

Monte Carlo police headquarters. Although the search proves fruitless, Trixie spots their attacker in a newspaper article about a Mr. Flashbucks, "a heavy winner at roulette." Police Inspector Anton Dubious, along with Speed and Trixie, pay Flashbucks a visit at his gaming table. Of course, he denies the accusation.

Later that night, Speed visits the gambler in his hotel room. Flashbucks admits he lied to the police. Speed kicks him and grabs his gun. A fight ensues. Running through the hotel, Speed is shot at but somehow escapes. Speed calls Inspector Dubious, confirming that Flashbucks is the criminal who attacked them. Before he can finish the conversation, he is knocked unconscious.

The next day, at the Grand Prix, Trixie, Spritle, and Chim Chim wait for Speed to show up. However, the race is canceled when the gas tanks suspiciously blow up. Flashbucks tells Speed, who is strapped to a wall, about his plan to blow up all the world's oil refineries. This would force everyone to ride trains and his investments in train stocks would soar.

Meanwhile, Sparky, Trixie, Spritle, and Chim Chim set out to rescue Speed. On a mountain road, they come to an enormous snow sculpture of the gambler. At his hideout, Flashbucks reiterates his scheme. Trixie sends the homing robot to knock a small bomb out of Flashbucks' hand. It is gobbled up by Chim Chim. Spritle releases Speed. The group escapes in the Mach 5. Speed grabs the bomb from Chim Chim's mouth and throws it out of the car. It explodes, destroying the hideout.

Episode 38: "The Secret Invaders (Part 1)"

When I mentioned going to the President's house, Racer X changed. Could he be a secret agent?

— SPEED RACER

In the "exotic and mysterious" city of Ambrocia, the Mystic Grand Prix is about to take place. Speed is driving Pops' new design, the Super-charged Formula 1. Princess Gracious, along with her husband, Prince Snowier, will signal the start of the race. A gunman lines up the Princess as his target. He misses the target, flees, and falls from a roof to his death.

In a train compartment, a member of Rudolph Elegantor's organization states he found a mirror on the racetrack. "Someone used it to flash light in our agent's eyes." He suspects one of the racers to be a secret agent: Rusty Muffle, Tailgate Crumple, or Speed Racer.

Speed and Trixie leave in the Mach 5 for Abalonia, site of the "hazardous" Twist 'n' Turn Race. After causing Rusty Muffle's car to crash and explode, Elegantor's men set upon Speed and Trixie. Racer X warns Speed that they are trying to kill him because they think he's a secret agent. Trixie asks where he is headed. Racer X replies, "If you must know, Paris."

In the city of love, the Chief of the International Secret Service speaks with Agent 8 (Tailgate Crumple) on his intercom. He tells Crumple to watch for Elegantor, but seconds later the agent is strangled by Elegantor. Elegantor has failed to take over Ambrocia. He decides to concentrate on Abalonia.

Speed, Trixie, Sprite, and Chim Chim arrive in Abalonia. They stop at a hotel. Speed gives his keys to a thug disguised as a parking attendant. Speed accepts an invitation to dine with President Montebank and leaves. Sprite and Chim Chim overhear the parking attendant/thug admit to sabotaging the Mach 5's tire. Using Trixie's transmitter, Sprite relays the information to Speed. Back at the hotel, the thugs chase Sprite and Chim Chim. Speed rescues them. Then, after a thug tells him a bomb is set to go off, he must rescue the President.

Episode 39: "The Secret Invaders (Part 2)"

Although Speed saved Montebank's life, both men have incurred injuries from the explosion. While they recuperate at National Hospital, a cowardly Vice President Duper and Rudolph Elegantor pay a visit to Montebank. But the doctor deems the President's condition "too serious to have visitors." While there, Elegantor decides to "pay a visit to the other victim," Speed Racer. He invites Speed to Duper's home. Racer X enters. After learning of Speed's visitor and the invitation, he hurries away to radio the Chief of International Police.

At Duper's home, Elegantor's thugs pull a gun on Speed. He is knocked unconscious, but later he leaves the house in the Mach 5. Racer X arrives. Finding that Speed has already left, he resumes his search. At the edge of a cliff, a thug peels away a Speed Racer face mask. The real

Speed Racer, still unconscious, is slumped over his steering wheel. A thug rolls the car off the cliff.

Reporters have gathered for Speed's funeral. Racer X spots Speed disguised in a trench coat and dark glasses. The two men vow to work together. A thug reports to Elegantor that Montebank will be vacationing in La Mamba. Elegantor tells Vice President Duper that once he is made President, "you will follow my orders." Racer X follows them all the way to La Mamba.

Duper and Elegantor arrive at Montebank's vacation residence. An assassination is attempted, but Montebank and his nurse turn out to be Speed and Trixie in disguise. A fight ensues. Elegantor throws Racer X out of the car. Stopping to pick up Duper, Elegantor speeds away. Eventually, the men struggle and the car swerves off a cliff. The next day, Speed and Racer X compete in the Twist 'n' Turn race.

Episode 40: "The Man behind the Mask"

Let me work as Dr. Fantasty's assistant. I can be very useful to him in the lab. Besides, from now on, I want to work for a winner. And I think you're clever enough to succeed in your plan to dominate the world. I want to be on your side from now on.

— SPEED RACER

Speed and Trixie are leaving for the North American Grand Prix. The Mach 5 is loaded onto an airplane along with a rocket. In flight, Speed meets

Dr. Fantasty, inventor of the rocket's fuel. Sprite and Chim Chim, who were found in the cargo area, are released into Speed's care. A man in a disfigured face mask takes the group to a "special secret island." Meanwhile, the Chief of the International Police confers with Agent 9 (Racer X) about the missing plane carrying Fantasty.

Mark Meglaton the Great greets Dr. Fantasty, Speed, and the gang. He takes them on a tour. He shows the group a room full of missiles, each "equipped with an anti-radar radar device" so it can travel undetected. "With this device, I can transport art treasures from anywhere in the world." Speed is ordered to collect the treasure and load it onto a rocket missile.

Meglaton orders Fantasty to develop "vast quantities" of his fuel. A "terrible" attack will be launched, forcing the world to surrender. Meanwhile, at the Racer homestead, Pops and Racer X vow to help Speed. On the road, Racer X jumps from a tree onto the Mach 5's hood. He disengages an explosive device, but Speed is lifted into Meglaton's plane. In another helicopter, Pops and Racer X set out in pursuit. Speed convinces Meglaton to let him be Fantasty's assistant. Later, Speed and Fantasty modify the engine into a ray gun and blast Meglaton and his soldiers. Fantasty launches the missiles, which turn around in flight and bomb the island instead. Speed finds Meglaton in the art gallery. He discovers that the man behind the mask is Fantasty's "best friend." At the North American Grand Prix, Speed ties for first place.

Episode 41: "The Car Destroyer"

So far we've gotten reports that 48,000 cars have disappeared with nobody driving them. Chief, there's only one person I know who might be able to get to the bottom of this. It's Speed Racer.

— INSPECTOR DETECTOR

Before the start of an auto race and before the drivers can get to their cars, the vehicles speed away. As the driverless cars leave the stadium, Dr. J. D. Crepit looks on with glee. Later, Crepit drives into an underground parking garage. From behind his license plate, a small ramp lowers and a fleet of miniature cars drives out, attaching themselves to the undersides of all the parked cars. By remote control, he has the parked cars follow him. Mean-

"I need someone to collect the art treasures for me, and I decided that Speed, who travels to races all over the world, would be the perfect one to carry out the job."
— MARK MEGLATON THE GREAT

"Trixie, the Mach 5 has been put under remote control of some kind. We're helpless!" — SPEED RACER

while, Inspector Detector turns the case over to Speed.

Before Speed can get started, Spritle sets out in a small truck to solve the mystery on his own. On the road, Spritle's truck drives away by itself. Speed passes the vehicle, then he turns around to follow it after Spritle and Chim Chim fall out of the back. The chase continues until they reach a castle. Suddenly, the Mach 5 is helpless. It, too, has been "put under remote control of some kind." The race car drives itself toward the castle and onto a conveyor belt leading to a fiery oven. Fortunately, the remote device is found and disconnected. At the foot of the castle, the gang comes upon a field of metal trees, flowers, and animals. Soon, the group is attacked by a tribe of miniature metal Indians and a fleet of miniature airplanes. Speed locates the projection room and confronts Crepit.

Crepit explains how he's getting revenge for the loss of his wife and the crippling of his son in an accident. But when his son enters in a wheelchair, he begs his father to stop. Speed and Crepit struggle. The son hoists himself up to grab Speed's arm, preventing him from striking his father. Crepit realizes the boy is standing. Speed points out "he was able to walk all along." Inspector Detector arrives to arrest Crepit.

Episode 42: "The Desperate Racer"

You're asking me to lose the Grand Prix? But that would be cheating and I've never done anything illegal in my life — ever!

— SPEED RACER

Speed, Trixie, and Sparky study a map of the Southern Hemisphere Pineapple Grand Prix. A young woman named Eloisa Hazard comes to the door. She asks Speed to lose the race so her brother, Hap, can win. Offended and angry, Speed orders her to leave and she faints. Speed drives her home and turns Eloisa over to her brother.

Later, Eloisa confides in Trixie. The prize money is needed to help make her well. But elsewhere, Hap is interrogated. A thug demands to know where Hap has hidden the King's jewel, known as the Mammoth Diamond. Hap confesses: It's hidden inside one of the pineapples to be used in the race.

On race day, each driver must carry a pineapple with him during the entire race. If the fruit is not with the winner at the finish, he will be

"If I don't keep this pineapple with me at all times, I'll be disqualified from the race. So, I'm sorry gentlemen, but you can't have it." — SPEED RACER

disqualified. The race begins. The thugs follow in an airplane. They "fish" the pineapples out of the race cars, slashing the fruit to find the stolen jewel. But time and again, they come up empty handed. Meanwhile, Speed is attacked by a gang of guitar-playing bandits. Hap accuses Speed of sending out men to steal his pineapple. Appalled, Speed reciprocates the accusation. The two men fight. Hap manages to steal Speed's pineapple. Determined to retrieve it, Speed chases him. Above, in her helicopter, Trixie begs Speed to let Hap win. Despite the plea, Speed accelerates and turns off the radio. Speed and Hap both get caught in a mud slide. Somehow the Mach 5 maneuvers out safely. Then, Speed tows Hap's vehicle. Suddenly, the thugs parachute to the ground and surround the racers. Speed and Hap fight them off. Speed retrieves his pineapple.

Speed wins the race. Quietly, Trixie tells Chim Chim to take Speed's pineapple to Hap's car. The baffled Speed is disqualified. Hap is proclaimed the winner of $10,000 and a ten-year supply of pineapples. A thousand smaller pineapples fall out of a piñata. The thugs dive in to find the jewel. But Chim Chim, in a feeding frenzy, bites into the jewel, then spits it out. Before the thugs can grab it, a police officer retrieves it. Hap and

Eloisa celebrate. Speed forgives Trixie for her prank.

Episode 43: "The Dangerous Witness"

You weren't hurt. Come on. Get up. You heard me. Stop faking.
— SPEED RACER, to the terrorist

On a plane headed for Hong Kong, Speed is witness to a woman firing a poisonous needle at a man in a nearby seat. When he confronts the woman, he sees that "she was hit by a needle the same as the man." Spritle notices something sticking out of the woman's purse. He hands it to his brother. It is an invitation to a famous floating restaurant. Close by, inconspicuously, Agent 9 (he's never identified as Racer X in this episode, probably because he's unmasked) and a menacing stewardess watch the scene.

At the airport, Princess Peddle's plane lands. Speed learns that she is one of the richest girls in the world. As Princess Peddle and her entourage pass, an unnamed woman opens her necklace containing a miniature missile and aims it at the Princess. But the assassination attempt is aborted when the stewardess tells the woman, "There's too much danger." Later, on a ferry boat, the captain is shot, taking a bullet meant for Speed. Chim Chim points to the culprit. A mysterious woman speeds away in a small boat.

Speed concludes the murders were not coincidences. Speed and Trixie hire a rickshaw to take them to the floating restaurant. A woman posing as a sword dancer aims the weapon at the Princess. Fortunately, Speed catches it in midair.

Later, Speed tells Trixie he has accepted the Princess's request to become her bodyguard. Then Trixie gets an idea. She disguises herself as a veiled Princess Peddle. Then, with her representative (Speed), the curator gives her a tour of a museum. Another assassination attempt is made. The woman flees in a red convertible. Speed chases her in the Mach 5. He slams into her car, causing it to crash. Nevertheless, the woman is able to pull a gun on him. Agent 9 appears to arrest her.

On race day, Speed is torn between racing and protecting the Princess. The race begins. Spritle points out driver X, who turns out to be the airline stewardess and the ringleader. While figuring this out, Speed notices that X is far behind the rest

"Now, destroy the car and everyone in it." — SLIMER

of the pack. The hood of her car opens and a rocket missile rises, aiming for Princess Peddle's box. Speed smashes into her car. Defeated, X admits that her "scheme failed."

Episode 44: "Race the Laser Tank"

We see how well the laser gun works on a stone wall and we'll see if it works against humans.
— SLIMER to Speed and Tanna,
a Secret Service agent

Speed wins the Eastern Central Grand Prix. Later that day, a man aims a camera at a young woman named Tanna. A bullet shoots from the camera. The target is missed when Speed and Trixie pull up alongside her vehicle. Speed is left believing the bullet was meant for him.

In Hawaii, Tanna gives Speed a lei as he steps off the plane. Spritle and Chim Chim, who have stowed away, hop on the back of a truck headed for Waikiki. The driver of the truck is hit by a bullet and the truck crashes. While Spritle and Chim Chim hide amid the wreckage, a man named Slimer and his thugs hover around the deceased driver. Unable to find what they're looking for, they leave. Spritle and Chim Chim sneak into the trunk of their car.

Speed and Trixie come upon the crash site. Trixie recognizes the truck. Later, Speed recognizes the deceased man. As Trixie pulls apart Speed's lei, a roll of microfilm falls to the floor. Speed goes to the library to find out what it contains. After skirmishes and chases, he discovers the construction site of a mysterious tank with several tentacles. He crashes off the mountain road, into the ocean.

Later, in a dungeon, Tanna wakes Speed. Slimer and his thugs enter the cell. Now that they have "the microfilm from that Secret Service girl," Slimer tells the pair they are going to be "guinea pigs" in a laser beam experiment. Just then, Spritle and Chim Chim climb out of the trunk and search for something to eat. They free Speed and Tanna.

The next morning, after blasting a hole through the cell wall with the laser, Slimer is ready to test his weapon on his human captives. Tanna kicks off her shoe, which doubles as a bomb, and they escape to the Mach 5. Slimer follows in a tank, but ultimately the vehicle falls into a volcano.

Episode 45: "The Great Car Wrestling Match"

Don't be stupid. Smashing cars on purpose is ridiculous. And anyone who does it shouldn't be allowed to drive a car.

— POPS RACER

The mysterious masked driver X (not Racer X) is proclaimed automotive wrestling champion. At the "famous" Universal Motor Show, Speed, Trixie, Sparky, and Spritle meet Gizmo and his father, whom Speed recognizes as Gag Zoomer, a profes-

sional race car driver. Spritle spots a camera on the floor. Speed volunteers to return it to Zoomer.

The next day, Speed speaks to a man from the Slip Shod Motor Company. He tells Speed that Zoomer was fired for losing "one of the big races." At the Zoomer homestead, Speed learns Zoomer is a car wrestler. Speed vows to stop the short-tempered man from car wrestling. He spots Zoomer at a gas station and follows him in the Mach 5 to a junkyard. After a crane lifts the Mach 5 high in the air, the car is released, and totaled.

Zoomer, disguised in his masked X costume, is taken to see his new car. A mechanic walks in with a message from Speed. He challenges Zoomer in the upcoming race.

Back at the garage, while Pops, Speed, and Sparky repair the Mach 5, Speed whispers to Trixie not to tell his father he has entered the car wrestling match. On race day, Speed smashes several cars by autojacking from one to the next.

Spritle and Gizmo meet in the stadium. On the track, there's a showdown between Speed and Driver X. The two cars collide in midair. Driver X's mask falls off. Gizmo runs to his father's aid. The boy begs his father to tell him he isn't a car wrestler. Speed arrives. He assures Gizmo, "your father came here to stop *me.*"

Episode 46: "Motorcycle Apaches"

They ride fast, heavily armed motorcycles and attack swiftly and then disappear into the hills. Their leader seems to be a young man with a wily genius and fierceness of what could be his ancestors — the dreaded Apache Indians in our early West.

— MR. SKYHIGH

Somewhere in "the American West," a tribe of motorcycle Apaches attack a convoy of trucks headed for the International Space Development Base. Nearby, Speed wins the Southwest Grand Prix. That evening Speed meets Mr. Skyhigh of the Office of Space Development. Skyhigh tells Speed of the attacks by the Apaches. Skyhigh asks Speed to deliver a vital load of Uraniumtane in the Mach 5.

Skyhigh informs Speed that a convoy will follow him. It will serve as a decoy to "trick the enemy." All the while, an Apache spies on the meeting. When he falls through the roof of an adjoining building, Spritle and Chim Chim come upon him and beat him up.

Skyhigh assigns Spritle and Chim Chim to deliver food to the base via covered wagon. It will take a different trail than Speed will. In the desert, the motorcycle Apaches surround the wagon. The Apaches try to steal the food, but Spritle and Chim Chim create such a commotion, the marauders abort the heist. They leave.

Meanwhile, an Apache spy radios his leader, Geronimo. Geronimo orders his tribe to assemble their weapons for a showdown. Determined to protect the load, the trucks form a circle around the Mach 5. Speed autojacks over the vehicles to escape. A duel between Speed in the Mach 5 and Geronimo on his motorcycle occurs. Ultimately, both vehicles crash. The box thought to contain the Uraniumtane falls out of the Mach 5; rocks spill out. Spritle and Chim Chim arrive at the Space Development Base. They learn they were carrying the Uraniumtane all along.

Episode 47: "Car with a Brain"

Dr. McFife was a brilliant scientist, and I believe he built and activated that monster car just before he went completely wacky.

— POLICE CHIEF

In Scotland, an old "retired" scientist named Dr. McFife waits for lightning to awaken his armadillolike monster tank. The tank comes to life. It plows through town, destroying everything in its path. From a hotel balcony, Speed, Pops, Trixie,

Sparky, Spritle, and Chim Chim spot the culprit. Speed hops into the Mach 5 and chases the tank through the city. Yet Speed passes out when the force of the tank's fiery exhaust twirls the Mach 5 into the air, causing it to crash.

Later, the Scottish army counterattacks unsuccessfully. From his jail cell, McFife bellows out, "No one can stop it, either." Pops supposes the tank is "being operated by a total built-in electronic brain." Speed suggests they attack while the tank is submerged. The police chief sends the navy submarines to attack. Speed drives the Mach 5 in after the tank. Speed notices a hatch in the tank's underbelly. Suddenly, the force of a ray-beam explosion propels the Mach 5 out of control, and Speed passes out.

The tank emerges from the water and continues its path of destruction. Speed tells of the hatch. He volunteers to plant an "electronic brain rattler" onboard the tank. Driving underneath the tank, Speed sends the homing robot to knock the door open. He autojacks the Mach 5 into its interior. Spritle and Chim Chim, stowaways in the trunk, climb out. Speed orders them all back into the

Mach 5. The race car is able to jump out of the tank. Stuck on a mountaintop, with nowhere to go, the tank blows up.

Episode 48: "Junk Car Grand Prix"

In his palatial mansion, Baron Von Vondervon announces that he will hold a Junk Yard Grand Prix in honor of his daughter, Yvonne Von Vondervon, who disappeared twelve years ago. The winner will receive money and be treated as if she were his own daughter. An old man comes forward to read the official rules. A man named Mr. Freeload assures a timid young woman named Lollie that, when she wins, she "might be more than rich." Freeload eyes the Baron's tie pin, a Superstar Topaz.

That evening, Speed gawks at a young woman repairing her automobile and is impressed with her mechanical skill. The girl wears an identical Topaz clip in her hair. On race day, Speed approaches the girl and learns that she and her entourage of children are orphans.

On the course, Freeload dons a scarf and

The Junk Yard Grand Prix

sideswipes every car he passes. He then radios a helicopter to shoot "sleep capsules" at Speed and Trixie. Another helicopter dives toward the orphans' car, but the copter crashes.

While the orphan girl recovers from the helicopter attack, a bunch of thugs ride up on horse-

Slash Marker Jr. sets out to avenge his father's death.

back, followed by Freeload in Lollie's car. When he realizes that the orphan girl must be the Baron's long-lost daughter, Freeload kidnaps the girl. Speed and Trixie learn what has happened. While Trixie resumes the race, Speed sets out in the Mach 5 to find the girl. After much fighting, Speed unties the orphan girl just as a thug enters with Trixie. Freeload offers to switch girls. But Chim Chim plants firecrackers in his pants. Freeload and his men are defeated. Trixie wins the race. The Baron reunites with his daughter, honoring her at a grand party.

Episode 49: "The Car in the Sky"

This is one tough spot the Mach 5 can't help us out on. If only I could use the car radio, but that was broken in the crash. And I don't know which direction to send the homing robot so that's out, too. And the cutters are useless. And the special wheels. Even the oxygen tank. No, I'm afraid the Mach 5 can't help us.

— SPEED RACER

On a stormy night, a bolt of lightning strikes an airplane, causing it to catch fire and crash on an uninhabited island. Pops discovers that the Mach 5 is a casualty while Trixie consoles a young woman named Suzie, who was on her way to see her sick mother. The group discovers an abandoned laboratory. Speed notices a crate with the logo "Ad-Baloon" stamped on it. He gets an idea to use the Mach 5 to make a "sort of makeshift dirigible." Because the Mach 5 can carry only three passen-

"Now listen carefully to my plan, everybody. We could hang the Mach 5 under a bunch of the advertising balloons and have sort of a makeshift dirigible."

gers, the group argues about who will go. Ultimately, Speed, a man named Mr. Bootis, and Suzie win.

In flight, Mr. Bootis is angry when Spritle and Chim Chim climb out of the trunk. Spritle apologizes. Speed tries to "lighten the load." He grabs Bootis's briefcase, which opens to reveal a fortune in gold bars.

Later, Speed notices they're out of gas. They must drift toward land. Bootis constructs a flying apparatus of his own, using a tire held by one of the balloons. However, his balloon crashes and explodes. Eventually, the dirigible drifts over the Grand Prix racing course. The crowd cheers as they sail past. As they head toward Suzie's mother's house, Speed instructs Chim Chim to parachute to land "to tell the search party about everyone on the island."

Episode 50: "The Trick Race"

Do you remember that race of a year ago, Speed? Think back and remember it well. How could you forget — hey? We will race you again — soon. Over the same treacherous trails. Over the same yawning chasm. Over the same breach of disaster. And we will BEAT YOU!

— Captain Terror

The surviving members of the Car Acrobatic Team meet high in the Bavarian Alps. Their leader, Captain Terror, vows not only to defeat Speed but to "destroy him." Late at night Speed dreams about the challenge. Upon waking, he hops into the Mach 5. Racer X stops him. He warns, "A race is not a fight."

Underneath an abandoned house, Mr. Supremo holds a board meeting of his International Spies, Incorporated. Mr. Magneato complains about Secret Agent Racer X. He identifies Speed as a problem, too.

Speed and Captain Terror meet and the race begins. Nearby, Racer X is shot at by Magneato's men. Eventually, Racer X learns a time bomb has been planted in all of the Car Acrobatic Team cars, set to explode once they surround Speed. Intent to rescue his younger brother, he manages to interrupt the race.

Captain Terror vows to help Racer X. Determined to "take their own bombs back to them," Captain Terror, Speed, and Racer X set out for the spy headquarters. They surround the hideout with the bomb-laden cars, then "run for their lives."

"Racer X. Are you my brother? Are you my brother, Rex racer?"

—*SPEED RACER*

The explosion is massive. Racer X is satisfied that "the countries of the world can have peace." In perhaps what is the most poignant moment of the series, Speed asks Racer X if he's his brother, Rex. Not willing to give away his identity, Racer X punches Speed in the stomach, knocking him out. As he drops his face mask next to his unconscious brother, he declares he's giving up being a racer "to be a full-time International Secret Agent without a name or a country." Speed finds Racer X's mask. Teary-eyed, he promises "to be the best racer in the world and to make you proud of your younger brother."

Episode 51: "Race Around the World (Part 1)"

SPEED: *All the gold in the world isn't worth a man's honor. That's the most precious thing there is.*

SHANE: *Out of what stupid book did you get that stupid idea? Little mister goody over there thinks he's smart with ideas like that.*

Mr. Karat Goldminter donates a "small mountain of gold" and his daughter, Lovelace, to the winner of the Around the World Grand Prix. But disguising herself as a boy, Lovelace insists she'll marry whom she pleases.

In a lounge, a driver named Scrounge points out a loophole in the rules. Speed presents his moralistic view about winning "fair and square and no other way." They fight. On race day, Sparky rides with Speed in an unidentified race car model, while Trixie, Pops, Spritle, and Chim Chim follow in the helicopter. Scrounge impedes other racers while Lovelace vows to teach her father a lesson. In Miami, the drivers switch to boats. Speed and Sparky jump into boat 5. Spritle and Chim Chim, who mistakenly have hidden aboard Lovelace's boat, overhear her say that "number 5 should have trouble any minute." Speed's boat catches fire. After being thrown overboard, Spritle paddles toward his brother and informs Speed of what has happened. Then, almost as recompense, Lovelace totals her speedboat on some rocks.

While Scrounge and his partner, Shane, speed past the shipwrecked team, Speed offers to help them. Lovelace refuses. Speed dives in the water, knife in mouth, to battle a shark to its death. The race resumes. A scuba diver drives up to Lovelace with a stolen boat. Reaching the Amazon River, Speed and Sparky set out to take the lead from Scrounge, whose boat flips over in an alligator pit. Then, Lovelace pulls into the lead. Speed drives his boat on land to avoid the alligators and to edge out Lovelace for first position. The race continues via propeller planes. Soon, Scrounge causes Speed's plane to crash in the jungle.

Episode 52: "Race around the World (Part 2)"

Speed and Sparky manage to jump out before their plane crashes. They build a log raft, then somehow they switch to a submarine and catch up to the other racers. At the South Pole, the two men climb aboard their "snow tracker" truck, determined to take the lead. Scrounge plows through a flock of penguins; Lovelace crashes into a deep gorge. Speed turns around to help. When they resume the race, Spritle whispers his discovery to his skeptical brother.

Lovelace "feels like a fool" for not thanking Speed. Then, going "from the cold of the South Pole to the terrible heat of the [Sahara] desert," Speed and Sparky survive hand grenades and a sand tornado on motorcycles. Once again, Scrounge sabotages the course. While Speed and Sparky hang from a cliff, Lovelace comes to the rescue. The race resumes with kayaks along the Rhine River.

In Russia, Speed and Sparky take off in the Mach 5 toward Siberia. Lovelace runs out of gas. Speed gives her his reserve. He hopes that will tell him "why a girl has entered this dangerous race." When Speed is stranded, Racer X comes on the scene. He reprimands Speed for helping his competitors. In Vladivostok, Scrounge and Lovelace's cars are loaded on a ship headed for the "last lap" in Tokyo. The race announcer reports that out of two hundred entries, only two cars remain. But, as the ship leaves the dock, Speed autojacks aboard.

In Japan, with only ten more miles to go, Speed leads. Scrounge crashes. Speed edges out Lovelace to become the World's Champion racing driver. Speed acknowledges Lovelace's true identity. Lovelace and her father forgive each other. Speed is honored in a ticker-tape parade. Racer X vows to keep an eye on his younger brother, "always." "He's the greatest racing driver in the world now, and he deserves the championship."

SPEED RACER CREDITS

Mach Go Go Go/Speed Racer

Fifty-two half-hour animated episodes produced by Tatsunoko Production Co., Ltd., Japan, 1966.

Broadcast History (Japan)
Fuji TV (Channel 8); 6:30 P.M. weekly,
April 2, 1967–March 31, 1968

Broadcast History (U.S.)
Syndicated (worldwide) beginning in September, 1967

Distribution History (U.S.)
Trans-Lux Television Corporation 1967–1969
Alan Enterprises 1969–1986
Color Systems Technology 1986–1989
Broadway Video 1989–1991
Speed Racer Enterprises 1992–present

Planned by:	Jinzo Toriumi
Executive Producer:	Hiroshi Sasagawa
Producer:	Tatsuo Yoshida
Chief Writer:	Jinzo Toriumi
Writers:	Jinzo Toriumi, Tadashi Hirose, Takashi Kusagawa
Chief Animator:	Masami Suda
Directed by:	Ippei Kuri, Hiroshi Sasagawa, Seitaro Hara
Chief Artist:	Mitsutaka Nakamura
Music by:	Nobuyoshi Koshibe
Sound Director:	Minoru Kimura

Special Effects:	Ishida Sound Productions
Recording Studio:	Yomihiro Studios
Filmed by:	Katsumi Matsushita
Photo Lab:	Toyo Photo Lab

Voices (Japan)
Yukiya Tanaka (Goh Mifune — Speed Racer)
Keiko Matsuo, Michiko Nomura (Michi Shimura — Trixie)
Kinya Aikawa (Kenichi Mifune — Racer X)
Teiji Omiya (Daisuke Mifune — Mom Racer)
Yoshiko Kimiya (Aya Mifune — Pops Racer)
Jyunko Hori (Kuri Mifune — Spritle)
Takashi Tomiyama (Sabu — Sparky)
Kenji Utsumi (Rokugo Keibu — Inspector Detector)
(Sanpei — Chim Chim, is not credited)

Voices (U.S.)
Peter Fernandez (Speed Racer, Racer X)
Jack Grimes (Sparky, Chim Chim)
Corinne Orr (Trixie, Spritle, Mom Racer)
Jack Curtis (Pops Racer, Inspector Detector)

English Adaptation Written and Directed by: Peter Fernandez
U.S. Production Coordinated by: Zavala-Riss Productions

U.S. Production Supervised by: K. Fujita Associates, Inc.

52 Laps around the Track

7

READY, SET, GO!

The *Speed Racer* Trivia Challenge

Choose the correct answer from the following choices:

1. What was the first race Speed entered?

a. The Sword Mountain Race
b. The Indy 500
c. The Big Alpine Race

2. Aside from the regular cast, who are the only characters to be featured in another story line?

a. The Gang of Assassins
b. The Car Acrobatic Team
c. The Motorcycle Apaches

3. Why did Racer X leave home?

a. Because Spritle gave him a headache.
b. Because he crashed Pops' car in a race and Pops chewed him out for not having enough experience and skill.
c. Because he accepted an offer to work as a secret agent for the International Police.

4. For what race did Speed earn the title World's Champion?

a. The Danger Pass Race
b. The Junk Car Grand Prix
c. The Around the World Grand Prix

5. How did Speed once lose his signature red scarf?

a. He gave it to an adoring fan.
b. A giant spider tore it off with its claw.
c. He used it to create a splint for a racer's injured leg.

6. What did horseman Mr. Trotter and retired scientist Dr. J. D. Crepit have in common?

a. They had daughters who wanted to become race car drivers.
b. They hated cars.
c. They wanted to ride in Speed's makeshift dirigible.

7. Who did Racer X secretly pose as?

a. Kabala
b. Captain Terror
c. Mark Meglaton the Great

8. How old is Speed?

a. 16
b. 18
c. 21

9. In the Around the World Grand Prix, what means of transportation did the competitors *not* use?

a. Hot air balloon
b. Submarine
c. Snow tracker

10. Where did Pops hide the plans for the redesign of the Mach 5's engine?

a. On the Mach 5's windshield with invisible ink
b. Etched on the Mach 5's engine
c. On microfilm hidden in the homing robot

11. When a plane crashed on an uncharted island, how did Speed set out for help?

a. He drove the Mach 5 on the bottom of the ocean.
b. He created a makeshift dirigible.
c. He sent a message in the homing robot.

12. When Speed and Kim Jugger raced each other without brakes, what did Ali Ben Schemer leave in each man's car?

a. a time bomb
b. a pineapple
c. a scorpion

Ready, Set, Go!

13. Who is Bent Cranium?

a. The man who invented the GRX engine
b. The man who invented the Mizmo Ray
c. The man who invented the Supersonic Rocket Car

14. What did race car driver Gag Zoomer and the Hong Kong stewardess have in common?

a. They were both known as X.
b. They had a fear of flying.
c. They were secret agents for the International Police.

15. What dangerous stunt did Twinkle Banks perform?

a. She drove a car on two ropes stretched across Niagara Falls.
b. She cleared the highest stack of cars in the Stunt Car Spectacular.
c. She raced her car tipped on two wheels.

16. Who owned the Mammoth Car?

a. Louis Towcar
b. Cruncher Block
c. Guts Buster

17. What kind of handicap challenged Delicia, the daughter of escaped convict Lawson Lamster?

a. She was deaf.
b. She was blind.
c. She was dumb.

18. What did one have to do before driving the GRX race car?

a. Inhale V Gas.
b. Drink water.
c. Fasten the seat belt.

19. What did the Chief of Kapecapek and Mr. Goldminter, the host of the Junk Yard Grand Prix, have in common?

a. They were exiles from Bangdabongo.
b. They named their daughters as a prize for the winner of a car race.
c. They were one-eyed men.

20. What was Speed asked to deliver to the International Space Development Base?

a. Intercontinental Ballistic Missiles
b. Uraniumtane
c. Rocket fuel

21. Aside from auto racing, what other kind of car sport did Speed once compete in?

a. A monster car championship
b. A go-cart championship
c. A car wrestling championship

22. What did Chim Chim find when he bit into a pineapple?

a. The King's jewel, called the Mammoth Diamond
b. A roll of microfilm containing plans for a laser beam
c. The Super Star Topaz

23. What did Slash Marker call his X3 race car?

a. The Speed Demon
b. The Melange
c. The Zodiac

24. Who was the leader of the Motorcycle Apaches?

a. Ug
b. Chief Black Hawk
c. Geronimo

25. What did Mark Meglaton the Great force Speed to steal?

a. Works of art around the world
b. Cleopatra's treasure
c. A pineapple

26. In a secret African laboratory, what was Professor Loon creating?

a. A flying submarine dragon
b. A car with a brain
c. Giant gorillas and bugs

27. What special device did Pops equip the Mach 5 with so as to enhance Speed's chances against the Car Acrobatic Team in the Big Alpine Race?

a. Wings
b. An infrared night scope
c. Belt grips for the tires

28. Who raced the GRX in the Oriental Grand Prix?

a. Speed
b. Louis Towcar
c. Curly Cranium

29. What did the Gang of Assassins and Junk Car Grand Prix competitor Mr. Freeload have in common?

a. They fired sleeping gas on their opponents.
b. They were employed by International Spies, Incorporated.
c. They were after $1billion in gold bars.

30. After Speed, Racer X, and the Car Acrobatic Team defeated Mr. Supremo and his unruly bunch from International Spies, Incorporated, Speed asked Racer X if he was his older brother, Rex Racer. What happened?

a. Racer X punched him in the stomach.
b. Racer X admitted his true identity and asked Speed to keep it a secret.
c. Racer X laughed and said he was only Speed's closest competitor, nothing more.

Answers

5. b	10. a	15. a	20. b	25. a	30. a
4. c	9. a	14. a	19. b	24. c	29. a
3. b	8. b	13. a	18. a	23. b	28. c
2. b	7. a	12. c	17. b	22. a	27. a
1. a	6. b	11. b	16. b	21. c	26. c

QUESTIONS *SPEED RACER* NEVER ANSWERS

DID YOU EVER WONDER...?

- What the true identity of Mr. Supremo, the head of International Spies, Incorporated, is?

- Where Trixie got the money to purchase a helicopter?

- Why Speed didn't recognize Racer X's voice as that of his brother?

- Why Speed didn't check the trunk to see if Spritle and Chim Chim were stowed away before he took off?

- Where Sparky and Trixie live?

- What Pops' first name is?

- Why Chim Chim wasn't quarantined at each international destination?

- If Speed and Trixie did it?

Ready, Set, Go!

8 NOW COMICS

Speed Mania Begins!

In 1985, long before *Speed Racer* made its comeback on MTV (in 1993), Tony Caputo, founder of NOW Comics, rescued the series from obscurity, bringing it back into the forefront of our collective minds. In total, sixty-six comic books were published (forty-five *Speed Racer,* and twenty-one *Racer X* comics) from 1987 to 1990, generating sales in excess of $2 million. Quite an accomplishment for a small company whose competition were the pinnacles of the comic book industry like Marvel, DC, and Comico.

At the time, Tony was an art director for a small Chicago ad agency. Combining his background in art with his love of comic books, he started out publishing a quarterly fanzine called *Fangraphix*, a collection of comics from people all over the country. A bimonthly, full-color, half computer-animated comic called *Vector* followed. "It was way ahead of its time," Tony reflects. "And then there was *Syphons*. That was a superhero comic." After a series of other minor successes, Tony realized that licensing intellectual properties

was the way to go. "I wanted to have [sales of] a half million like every other publisher."

As with most successful entrepreneurs, what began as a hobby turned into a full-time enterprise. Soon, Tony quit his job, and he and his then wife, Nanette Injeski, moved the company off their dining room table and into an office suite on Chicago's prestigious Michigan Avenue. "I noticed there was a big surge in independent publishers. And I learned immediately that as soon as you go into publishing comics, you go into competition with Marvel and DC because you're fighting for the same talent, the same shelf space, and the same consumer dollars. So, it dawned on me that although I couldn't buy the thirty-year history Marvel had or the sixty-year history DC had, I could buy *recognition*. Comico was publishing *Robotech* and they were selling 100,000 copies a month. There was a big Japanese animation craze and I thought that *Speed Racer*, being the most popular Japanese animated series in America, would do great. I also looked at [and eventually bought] the rights to *Astro Boy*."

While *Astro Boy* was purchased directly from Suzuki Associates International, Inc., in

Japan, the rights to *Speed Racer* were eventually negotiated by Columbia Pictures. "It's a funny story," Tony recalls. "My negotiations started with Alan Enterprises. But around 1986, negotiations came to a halt because Color Systems Technology (known for colorizing old TV shows and movies) bought out Alan Enterprises. Negotiations started again, but about a month later, they told me to wait. So, after a couple of weeks, Color Systems told me to talk to Coca-Cola Telecommunications because they had purchased Color Systems. Then, I was told to talk to Columbia Pictures Merchandising (Coca-Cola at that time owned Columbia Pictures). And that's where I signed the contract. I purchased the rights for $1,000 and 5 percent of receipt royalties." (The license would change hands again to Broadway Video before finally resting at Speed Racer Enterprises.)

Tony realized the gold mine he had during the spring of

*A page from Speed Racer,
NOW Comics © 1988*

1987 at the Diamond Trade Show (the largest worldwide distributor of comic books) in Orlando, Florida. "At a small booth *Speed Racer* and *Astro Boy* were presented with our display and everyone went absolutely bonkers. All the publishers were looking [to acquire] these properties.

"My idea was not to necessarily do *Speed Racer* like the cartoon. I hadn't seen it since I was seven or eight years old. I got a couple of tapes from Columbia and I couldn't stop laughing because all those images and excitement came back to me. And, I'm saying, 'Oh my God, it's *Speed Racer*!' It was so corny and goofy. We didn't want people to just buy the first issue because of the nostalgia. So, we tried to modernize him but keep the integrity. There's a lot you can get away with on a cartoon that you can't get away with in print. Like they never explained why he was named Speed Racer. We decided Greg Racer was his real name. It had to do a lot with Greg from *The Brady Bunch*. I always thought Greg Brady could be Speed Racer. And we gave him a fireproof jumpsuit instead of the scarf and bellbottoms. The fans loved it."

Other answers to questions long boggling our minds were provided. Like, where exactly did the Racers live? (In Farmington Hills, Michigan. But soon the clan moves to San Francisco.) Why is there a large age gap between the Racer boys? (Rex and Greg are adopted, as is Spritle later on.) Where do Sparky and Trixie live? (Sparky lives above the Racers' garage; Trixie lives in San Francisco's Clairmont Hotel.) And who's the president of the Race Car Association? (Kentucky Fried Chicken's Colonel Sanders, of all people!)

In total, about twenty-five freelance artists and writers worked on the comics. "In the beginning we had a joke about it having the artist curse. It seemed there wasn't an artist committed to the book (and this was all before computers). Finally, we hired Norm Dwyer, who stayed for a couple of years. And Len Strazewski did a great job of capturing [the essence of] each script. It was fun to do. There was no other book that I published, including *The Real Ghostbusters*, *Terminator*, and *The Green Hornet*, that got more mail than *Speed Racer*."

Not wanting the *Speed Racer* and *Astro Boy* comics to compete against each other, Tony had the first *Speed Racer* comic debut the weekend of July 4, 1987, on the eve of the Chicago Comic Convention. *Astro Boy* followed a month later. Designed for the more "sophisticated" crowd, the *Racer X* series hit the stands a year later in June of 1988. "There are things you can do with Racer X that you can't do with Speed. For example, we didn't think it was a good idea for Speed to kill somebody for no reason. In self-defense it was okay. *Racer X* was darker, and we actually had fans that didn't know *Speed Racer*, the TV series, existed." (The show wasn't syndicated to every U.S. market or to Canada.)

Ultimately, over 100,000 copies of *Speed Racer* issue #1 were distributed worldwide (95% in the United States, 3% in Canada, and the remaining 2% to overseas U.S. military stations). Initially, 50,000 copies were printed, "but at the Chicago Comic Convention, every single dealer came up to me asking for more copies because they were selling like crazy," says Tony. "One retailer said he bought 500 copies because he knew it was going to be hot. That was three times what he had bought for *X-Men*. The one thing I noticed about *Speed Racer* that was unique was that it introduced new life into the comic book industry. New people were brought in that have never bought a comic book in their life. That's why the comic book industry went from an annual $140 million business in 1985 to a $1.5 *billion* business in 1992. *Speed Racer* was one of the many books responsible for that."

Aside from publishing comic books, Tony also got permission from Nippon Books in Japan to reprint the Japanese "Speed Racer" *manga* by Tatsuo Yoshida. Translated into English, two volumes were published and titled *Speed Racer Classics*. By popular demand, twenty-two videotape volumes containing two unedited "Speed Racer" episodes per tape were sold exclusively through mail order. (Although these videos are no longer for sale, Family Home Entertainment currently sells twelve videotapes, also comprised of two unedited episodes each. If you *must* have all fifty-two episodes, you'll have to tape those you are missing off the Cartoon Network, or trade with friends.)

Unfortunately, as the year 1995 came to a close, so did NOW Comics. Although Tony left in 1994, a decision due in part to the restructuring of new investors and waning video sales, his partners manned the helm for an additional year. "It has been the highlight of my life," says Tony. "I just wish the rights had been straightened out back then."

A VOTE FOR SPEED

In 1988, when David Lane Seltzer first started making noise about producing a live-action version of *Speed Racer* for Warner Bros., NOW Comics readers submitted their vote for the cast. And the winners were . . .

Speed Racer: Charlie Sheen, Tom Cruise, Johnny Depp, Michael J. Fox

Racer X: Tom Cruise, Kyle MacLachlan, George Michael, David Hasselhoff, Nick Mancuso, Dennis Quaid

Pops Racer: Dick Butkus, Mike Ditka, William Conrad

Mom Racer: Amanda Page, Gates McFadden, Meredith Baxter-Birney, Kathleen Turner, Jane Fonda, Raquel Welch, Sally Field, Joanna Kerns

Spritle: Benji Gregory, Lukas Haas, Brian Bonsall

Chim Chim: Bubbles (Michael Jackson's pet), the chimp who played "Virgil" in Project X

Trixie: Alyssa Milano, Tracey Gold, Valerie Bertinelli, Phoebe Cates, Ally Sheedy, Tahnee Welch, Nancy McKeon, Molly Ringwald

Sparky: Pee Wee Herman, Wil Wheaton, Michael Keaton, Ricky Schroder

9

SPEED REVS UP THE BIG SCREEN

The Speed Racer Show

Give a round of applause to Carl Macek and Jerry Beck. They're the team who, in 1993, created the eighty-minute feature, *The Speed Racer Show*. Shown mostly in "art" theaters and on college campuses nationwide, the film is comprised of three episodes from the original series, and it was an instant sell-out hit. It debuted the summer of 1993. Four years later, it continues to pick up bookings. But, if you haven't been lucky enough to watch it along with hundreds of enthusiastic fans, don't worry — it's available on video retitled as *Speed Racer: The Movie*, distributed by Family Home Entertainment.

Two lifelong fans of animation, Carl and Jerry formed Streamline Pictures, a Los Angeles-based company devoted to distributing Japanese

animation to movie theaters and video. Jerry, now vice president, Animation, for Nickelodeon Movies, recalls, "It was like a cause. We both believed animation is more than just a babysitter for kids as it's believed to be in this country. It's not that way in Japan. They have kids' stuff and they have adult cartoons. We just wanted to raise the consciousness of America."

And so they did. In fact, it wouldn't be an exaggeration to credit them for opening the floodgates, making Japanese animation readily available in the United States. Pre-1990, "the only way to get Japanese cartoons was to get bootleg copies, or to trade with someone from Japan." Now, in video stores nationwide, whole sections are devoted to selling *anime*.

In 1987, Carl and Jerry conceived their partnership at the Animation Celebration. It was held at the Wadsworth Theatre, adjacent to the UCLA campus, and it was Jerry's job to help compile the world-class animated shorts for the festival. Afterward, while the Who's Who of the animation industry were wined and dined at a party outside, about two thousand teens and adults were inside enjoying the late-night "Japanimated" screening of *Robotech the Movie*. "It was really cool," Jerry remembers. Carl, who was hired by Harmony Gold to dub the series into English, was also there.

"The next few months we talked more and more about the idea of talking to Japanese companies to distribute their animation. We visited Japanese animation studios that had offices in Los Angeles, presenting ourselves as Streamline Pictures." All in all, the team released about ten Japanese feature films into American theaters (video distribution soon followed). These include *Lensman*, *Robot Carnival*, *Wicked City*, *Fist of the North Star*, and their jewel in the crown, *Akira*.

Amid the merchandising bonanza created by John and Jim Rocknowski, who bought

the worldwide rights to the *Speed Racer* series, Jerry and Carl bought the theatrical rights from them.

"In 1992, *Speed Racer* was becoming very popular for some reason. People were being nostalgic, so I felt the time was right," says Jerry. "My first reaction was that I didn't think a *Speed Racer* movie was going to work. But since I was going to be selling it to theaters, I had to really believe in it. The Rocknowskis gave us a copy of all fifty-two episodes, and I figured we should use one of the two-parters so it would feel more like a movie. I

Nuart Theater: June 1993

Speed Revs Up the Big Screen

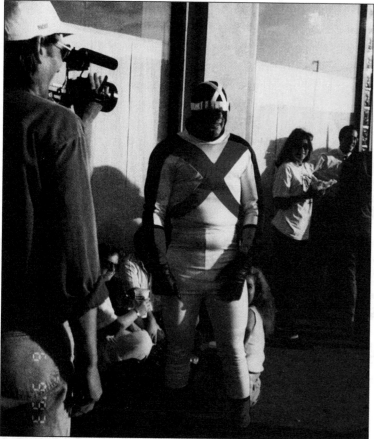

Will the real Racer X please come forward?

would have to put Racer X in because people would be expecting it. I looked at all the episodes and thought that people always remembered the Mammoth Car episodes."

The project took a couple of months to put together. Duplicate negatives of the original 35mm print of the episodes were obtained from Tatsunoko Productions in Japan. Jim Rocknowski had a negative for the opening sequence that turned out to be the original Japanese opening (without sound) in a Los Angeles warehouse. These were edited together and matched up to an "Americanized" 16mm print. However, the Japanese version had more footage. Since the sound of the shorter American print had to sync up with its longer counterpart, sound bites were taken from other parts of the show and used to fill in the gaps. "Sometimes we had to add a sound effect here and there," Jerry recalls.

The opening presented more of a problem. Because the Americanized theme song was not long enough to cover the footage of the Japanese opening, Jerry opted to use a hybrid by combining some of the original theme with a grunge rock version recorded in 1992 by the Alpha Team. In retrospect, Jerry admits he should have used a version by Matthew Sweet, which kept the integrity of the original theme.

Since the episodes were formatted to accommodate commercials, the team contracted to use vintage ads from the era. In total, five versions, all with different commercials, were created. The home video release includes ads for "Bondex

remembered, as a film collector, I had a 16mm print of 'The Car Hater' episode. I always loved that one because I had shown it to people at parties and comic book conventions and it always got a great response because it started out explaining how the car worked. And then, it was also about a man who hated cars. It was campy and people laughed at it in a nostalgic way. So I thought this and something else would be great. And I knew I

Cement Paint," "Smokey the Bear," "New Flint House and Garden Insect Killer," and "Old King Cole" milk cartons. In addition, a "Colonel Bleep" short, "The Treacherous Pirate," was positioned before the start of the Mammoth Car episodes.

Although *The Speed Racer Show* made its debut in San Diego, the real debut occurred a couple of weeks later on June 9, 1993, at Santa Monica's Nuart Theater. The line of anxious fans formed an hour before the start of the show. While a man in a Racer X costume entertained the ever-lengthening line, local radio personality Richard Blade (KROQ 106.7 FM) added to the frenzy and served as the show's official host. However, the greatest moment occurred when the audience was introduced to the voices behind their childhood heroes, Peter Fernandez (voice of Speed and Racer X) and Corinne Orr (voice of Trixie and Spritle), who were flown out from New York for the event. Afterward, they signed specially created *Speed Racer* movie posters, and just about anything else put in front of them.

"I think we did a good job," Jerry reflects. "If I were coming to see that show, I would have thought they were just going to run some old episodes. But we ran what I consider to be some kind of movie."

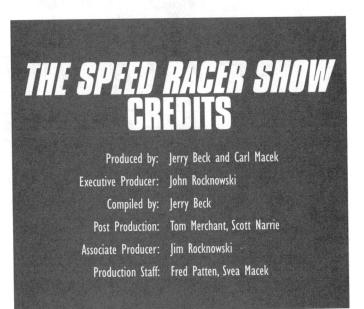

THE SPEED RACER SHOW CREDITS

Produced by:	Jerry Beck and Carl Macek
Executive Producer:	John Rocknowski
Compiled by:	Jerry Beck
Post Production:	Tom Merchant, Scott Narrie
Associate Producer:	Jim Rocknowski
Production Staff:	Fred Patten, Svea Macek

SPEED RACER JOINS NASCAR

The American phenomenon of NASCAR auto racing is big, and its popularity increases every year. According to ESPN's Director of Advertising Neal Tiles, NASCAR (the National Association of Stock Car Auto Racing) has surpassed horse racing as the number-one attendance sport. NASCAR's Winston Cup circuit drew 5.3 million fans to thirty-three events in 1995. Television ratings are also up. Broadcast on CBS, ABC, ESPN, TNN, and TBS, the races have posted a significant gain over 1995.

So when the advertising gurus at ESPN sat down in January 1996 to discuss how to attract new fans, "our main challenge," Neal recalls, "was to try to appeal to a new group of fans without alienating the current ones. That's hard." A few weeks later, ESPN's creative team, Tony Kobylinski and Jim Ritterhoff, presented Neal

with a few ideas, one of which included using the original *Speed Racer* cartoon. "My eyes went up because I knew *Speed Racer* was a big thing. It was part of the pop culture and I knew of the recent advertising success others had had with the whole retro-70s thing. It instantly struck a chord. *Speed Racer* was just campy enough. [The series] was an important part of our lives, and we kind of forgot about it because no one had reminded us of it."

Initially, clips from the original series were going to be edited together to tell a story; the voice-over remixed. "I liked the idea, but we thought we should try to give it a different angle than total animation. So we thought about Speed becoming a NASCAR driver. And the reason for that was, if we did it all animation, the NASCAR fan might say, 'What are you doing to my sport?' And we didn't want to alienate our fans. Plus, as a way to appeal to the NASCAR viewers, we thought we should include real drivers so that they could relate to it."

Next, Brian Buckley and Frank Todaro, the directing team at @radical.media,inc. were hired to make the series (of what would amount to ten 30-second spots) come to life. Brian recalls, "NASCAR was kind of afraid of letting the story take over the drivers. Speed, being such a celebrity, was overpowering the other guys. NASCAR's objective was to have Speed secondary, but as far as we were concerned, creatively, Speed was the key. The supporting cast were the race car drivers."

In an example of art imitating life (or maybe life imitating art), it was eventually settled that real NASCAR drivers would talk about Speed Racer as if he were a real person, not a cartoon character. Jeff Gordon (1995's Winston Cup champion) and Dale Earnhardt (who has won a total of seven Winston Cup championships and is ranked twentieth on Forbes' 1995 list of the forty top-paid athletes, with $8.4 million in earnings) were shoo-ins. Not only are they heroes of the current racing fans, they are probably the most recognizable names to general sports fans. "They were really gotta-have guys for the ads," says Neal. "And we needed Lake Speed because he is one of the drivers who is big on the tour, and we also wanted to play on his name."

Technically, the spots were a nightmare to shoot. Filmed during the North Wilkesboro race in April 1996, the directors (Brian and Frank) were faced with the deafening roar of dozens of cars (which are built without mufflers), thousands of excited spectators, and the distracted drivers themselves. "The main objective was to survive," Brian recalls. "We shot there for three days — two qualifying race days and one race day. The noise was mind-boggling. We would be in the middle of a spot and some guy would tune up his engine and we'd lose all audio. The drivers were doing the spots in between races, or just after having raced, or they had a few minutes until they had to qualify. Literally, we sometimes only had them for three to four minutes."

In total, the ads ran April through December, 1996. Kevin Triplett, ESPN's manager of communications, ponders, "It's hard to tell if the ratings went up because of the *Speed Racer* campaign. I would like to think that the effort we put into it and the uniqueness of the ads had some effect."

Nevertheless, be it on the Winston Cup circuit or driving above or below water, Speed reigns on the raceway.

BOBBY LABONTE

Personal Stats: 33, married, one son

Cars: Interstate Batteries Pontiac (has a total of ten cars)

Car Manufacturer: Pontiac; Joe Gibbs, owner (a former coach of the Washington Redskins; in 1995 his auto racing team won the Coca Cola 600; in 1993, the Daytona 500)

Pit Crew: 45; Jimmy Makar, Crew Chief

Engine Type: Small Block Chevrolet 357

Engine Cylinders: 8

Horsepower: 720

RPM: 8,500

Top Speed: 195 mph

Special Devices: Modified braking system, rear-end gearing cooler, protective roll cage, protective fuel cell, special duct work for oil cooler and radiator, fire-resistant uniform, air tube funnels that pump fresh air into the helmet, driver window safety net, in-car camera mounted behind driver

Passenger Space: None (no trunk)

Top Win: 1996 NAPA 500, Atlanta

Career Winnings: $3.7 million

Longest Race: Coca Cola 500, Charlotte (600 miles)

Most Difficult Track: North Wilkesboro Speedway, North Carolina (dropped from schedule beginning in 1997)

Most Challenging Opponents: His brother, Terry Labonte (1996 Winston Cup Champion); Dale Earnhardt

Street Wheels: 1996 Chevy pickup truck

Credo: "Never give up."

Idol: Speed Racer

Fallback Career: Crew member

*Bobby Labonte's car
(Interstate Batteries Pontiac)*

VS. SPEED RACER

SPEED RACER

Personal Stats: 18, single

Cars: Mach 5, Formula 1, Supersonic Rocket Car (Speed is also proficient in racing a speedboat, propeller boat, propeller plane, "snow tracker" truck, "ice yacht," log raft, motorcycle, and a kayak.)

Car Manufacturer: Pops Racer Motors; Pops Racer, owner

Pit Crew: Pops Racer, Sparky, Trixie

Engine Type: GOV12ENGINE

Engine Cylinders: 12

Horsepower: 20,000

RPM: 30,000

Top Speed: 155 mph

Special Devices: Auto jacks, grip tires, rotary saws, deflector shield, ultra-illuminating headlights, infrared goggles, underwater oxygen supply, periscope, homing robot, winglets

Passenger Space: 1 passenger seat; room for two in trunk

Top Win: World's Champion driver; the Around the World Grand Prix

Career Winnings: Unknown, but he won $5,000 in the Sword Mountain Race before Pops permitted him to become a professional race car driver

Longest Race: Around the World Grand Prix, 25,000 miles on land and water

Most Difficult Track: Yawning Chasm Pass on the Big Alpine racecourse

Most Challenging Opponents: Racer X (only we know he is Speed's brother); Captain Terror and his Car Acrobatic Team

Street Wheels: Mach 5

Credo: "I can win races fair and square."

Idol: Racer X

Fallback Career: Special Assistant to Inspector Detector

The Mach 5

Script A

Open on various NASCAR drivers going about their race preparations. Each is responding to the question of Speed Racer's imminent arrival on the NASCAR scene. Mixed in is footage from the original *Speed Racer* cartoon.

BILL ELLIOT: How will the other drivers react to Speed Racer? Good, I imagine. I mean the guy's a legend.

DALE EARNHARDT: Speed Racer's a joke. He's a cartoon.

LAKE SPEED: Don't know much about him. Like the name, though.

JOHN ANDRETTI: You have to take him seriously. He's never lost a race.

JEFF GORDON: Lot of guys'll tell you Speed's the reason they got into racing.

ERNIE IRVAN: He's got the car. That's for sure.

RICKY CRAVEN: It's tough being a rookie, but Speed's been around.

DALE EARNHARDT: (Reprise) He gets that Mach 5 too close to me, I'll make him pay.

Script B

Open on a garage late at night. NASCAR officials are tirelessly poring over blueprints and color photographs of the Mach 5 to make sure it fits within NASCAR guidelines. One of the officials is thumbing through the rule book.

OFFICIAL A: Let's go over it again . . . the bulletproof glass is okay . . . the automatic jacks, maybe . . . but the rotary saws are gonna have to go. What about the periscope and the homing robot?

OFFICIAL B: Technically, there's no rule against them.

OFFICIAL A: Enginewise?

OFFICIAL B: Enginewise, the guy's driving a rocket ship. NASA might clear it, but I'm not sure NASCAR can.

OFFICIAL A: How 'bout the monkey?

OFFICIAL B: Well, he's got precedent on his side there. Remember the guy back in '85 who drove with his parrot?

OFFICIAL A: Oh yeah.

COMMERCIAL CREDITS

Client ESPN

Neal Tiles, director of advertising

Tony Frere, producer

Tony Kobylinski, art director

Jim Ritterhoff, copy writer

Eric Heimbold, assistant producer

Production Company

@radical.media,inc.

Brian Buckley, director

Frank Todaro, director

Jon Kamen, executive producer

Gregg Carlesimo, producer

Thomas O'Malley, production manager

Dick Gordon, editor

Post Production

Red Car Hollywood

Jonathon Del Gatto, editor

Speed Racer Joins NASCAR

SPEED REVS UP
THE SMALL SCREEN

"Huh? The Volkswagen GTI?"

Volkswagen GTI poster

WITH THE MACH 5 SABOTAGED, THERE WAS ONLY ONE WAY SPEED COULD WIN THE RACE...

Speed in Volkswagen GTI commercial

The minute Japanese script at the bottom of the screen translates to: "Produced for Volkswagen of America by Arnold Communications and J. J. Sedelmaier Productions, 1996." At the racetrack, Speed announces to the regular cast of characters (sans Racer X) that "the Mach 5 has been sabotaged!" Inspector Detector arrives and hands Speed the keys to a red GTI. "Huh? The Volkswagen GTI?" A checkerboard wipe takes the viewer to the race. Trixie, from the passenger seat, urges Speed on. Cars clank. Speed swerves to avoid colliding with his competitors, who crash through the guardrail. Speed crosses the finish line and wins. "This GTI is amazing!"

The next scene shows an exuberant Pops and Sparky in the back seat of the GTI. Pops responds, "And it's got room for four!" The ubiquitous stowaways, Spritle and Chim Chim, pop up exclaiming, "Make that six!" While a modernized version of the *Speed Racer* theme song plays, Speed recites the campaign's tag line: "On the road of life there are passengers and there are drivers." Speed drives the GTI toward the viewer and hops out of the vehicle. He freezes in his infamous "go" position. The Volkswagen logo and "Drivers Wanted" appear over a white background to close the spot.

Many of you may have been surprised by the Volkswagen GTI commercial — the one featuring Speed Racer that made its debut during the 1996 Olympics. If Volkswagen sought to break through the clutter of Olympic advertising, it succeeded — at breakneck speed. The nostalgic characters and the stilted "Japanimation" clearly stood out amid its slick competitors, reinforcing Volkswagen's image to its target audience of those in their twenties and thirties: people who not only grew up with the show but also enjoy driving. What better way to showcase their "Drivers Wanted" campaign than by using the ultimate driver, Speed Racer?

The commercial opens with the Mach 5's spinning tire; "Sabotage" is superimposed over it.

Speed Revs Up the Small Screen

The 30-second animated commercial directed by J. J. Sedelmaier titled "Sabotage" garnered *Shoot* magazine's (a commercial industry news weekly) "Top Spot of the Week" and the 1996 Annie Award for best promotional spot. Founded in 1991, J. J. Sedelmaier's production company, based in White Plains, New York, "won" the account from Arnold Communications (Volkswagen's ad agency), beating out two other animation companies.

Initially, Sedelmaier wasn't told who the account was for. "And I couldn't tell him it was *Speed Racer,* either," says Arnold Communications' producer, Bill Goodell. "We were looking to do an animated commercial in the style of 60s Japanese animation. The next day on my desk, I get an hour-long cassette of a whole bunch of different things he pulled for reference: *Astro Boy, Speed Racer,* and other things. He sent me an animation guide that had historical articles about all the different cartoons, including *Speed Racer.* So immediately his enthusiasm and his passion for doing something in that period got my attention." Sedelmaier confirms, "I had not been smitten by a project like this in a long time."

"The schedule was not very luxurious," Sedelmaier recalls. "We had to deliver at least one week prior to its scheduled air date, the first Sunday of the Olympics. We got [the project] on May 3 and we finished on July 12 [1996]." Working with Lance Jensen and Alan Pafenbach, Arnold's creative team who developed the concept and story line, Sedelmaier set out to capture the essence of *Speed Racer.* "In the past two years, we've done a lot of work where we've essentially fooled the

viewer into thinking they're seeing something old. *Speed Racer* has quite a following. And if you can fool the cult followers, you are really getting away with something," Sedelmaier told *Shoot.* Unlike the ESPN spots where footage and sound bites were lifted from the original series, the animation, music, and effects were all created from scratch. Having viewed hours of the original episodes helped the team to keep the "look" and integrity of the show intact.

However, Sedelmaier did pay homage to the series by using Corinne Orr, the original voice of Trixie and Spritle. Billy West served as the voice of Speed, Pops, and Inspector Detector. Goodell says the exclusion of Peter Fernandez, the original voice of Speed and Racer X, was a matter of not knowing how "to get a hold of him."

Once the animation was completed, bi-coastal Elias Associates recreated the music and effects. Goodell recalls, "We wanted to update the *Speed Racer* soundtrack, but we didn't know exactly which direction to take it. Whether it should be rock and roll, contemporary, or respecting the original. After going round and round and working with Ron [Lawner, Arnold's chief creative officer], Lance, Alan, and Elias we decided to score it like it was the original TV show."

From the beginning, Sedelmaier planned to make the spot appear "old." "We didn't want to do, like, scratches or dirt because that's not what you see when you watch the show. You do see a lot of film grain. We shot it on 35mm film and had a print made and a negative from that. And I took it down to another print from that negative." Goodell adds, "We didn't want to degrade the image too much because it's going to be playing on the Olympics. So we still wanted to have great colors and not look all washed out."

In addition, Sedelmaier mixed the spot out of sync intentionally. "[Audio] would call me and say that the lips had not matched up, and I tried to explain that it's Japanese animation, but they didn't get it."

Arnold Communications pays tribute to themselves on the GTI's license plate: LARB101 — Lance, Alan, Ron, Bill. The number 101 is the agency's street address in Boston.

THE VOLKSWAGEN GTI COMMERCIAL CREDITS

Client: Volkswagen

Production Company

J. J. Sedelmaier Productions, White Plains, N.Y.

J. J. Sedelmaier, director/producer/editor

David Wachtenheim, head animator

Dean Lennert and Tom Warburton, animators

Mike Wetterhahn, assistant animator/airbrush

Jason Edward, assistant animator

Irene Cerdas, production coordinator

Gideon Kendall, backgrounds

Agency

Arnold Communications, Boston, Mass.

Ron Lawner, chief creative officer

Bill Goodell, associate director/broadcast production

Meredith Maloney, associate producer

Lance Jensen, associate creative director/copywriter

Alan Pafenbach, associate creative director/art director

Post Production

Tape House Digital, New York

Kevin Brown, editor

Transfer at The Tape House Editorial Co., New York

John Crowley, colorist

Mixed at Photomag, New York

Carl Mandelbaum, engineer

Music: Elias Associates, bicoastal

Alex Lasarenko and Fritz Doddy, composers/arrangers

103

The New Adventures of Speed Racer

In an attempt to cash in on nostalgia and develop a new audience of *Speed Racer* fans, Fred Wolf, president of Fred Wolf Films, obtained a license for the animated property from Santa Monica, California–based Speed Racer Enterprises in 1992, following years of legal entanglements. A year later, *The New Adventures of Speed Racer* hit the airwaves, debuting the week of September 13, 1993. Distributed domestically by Group W Productions, the thirteen half-hour cartoons were broadcast in more than 80 percent of the country, including all top twenty-five television markets. Abroad, Westinghouse International sold the show to over eighty countries. Unfortunately, the success of this much anticipated revival was short-lived.

The problem with *The New Adventures of Speed Racer* is two fold. First, if Fred Wolf sought to lure longtime fans who grew up with the show, he failed miserably. By replacing the "classic" show's theme song with a completely different rock 'n' roll composition (by Dennis C. Brown), the notion of striking a responsive chord and pass-

ing along the excitement to one's offspring was immediately squelched from the get-go. At the very least, creating an updated version of the original melody seemed warranted, even mandatory. Without going into detail, Fred cites "entanglements" as the reason for not using the original theme. In addition, "We elected not to do the same theme because, although it was campy and a cult thing, it didn't go with the new series."

That said, the second faux pas has to do with not keeping the integrity of the classic *Speed Racer*. While it's almost impossible to duplicate a masterpiece, especially after twenty-five years and employing different animation styles and techniques, no attempt to capture the *tone* and *look* of the original was made. The characters are almost unrecognizable, both visually and audibly. Speed is more stocky than lean and buff; Trixie went blonde; and Sparky sounds like an old man. Only Racer X resembles his classic counterpart. The Mach 5, well, it looks like a Toyota.

Other differences set apart *The New Adventures of Speed Racer* from its predecessor. While *Speed Racer* was scheduled in early evening in its Japanese homeland, a time period meant for family viewing, *The New Adventures of Speed Racer* was intentionally geared toward viewers age two to eleven. It was subsequently broadcast in early morning or afternoon time periods. Because of its target audience, the revival joined the ranks of most of the other mindless children's fare. Simply, the *Speed Racer* entity was downgraded to *cartoon*. The cartoony music, goofy sound effects, and silly plot situations truly made an unfortunate

experience for any classic enthusiast. In fact, Kenji Yoshida, *Speed Racer*'s original producer, now president of Tatsunoko Studios, bowed his head in silence when asked how he felt about Wolf's rendition. It is these aspects that led to the revival's early demise. Even a five-year-old recognizes and remembers quality.

Nevertheless, it was produced and some credit should be given for introducing Speed and his friends to a new legion of fans. At the time, when shows such as *X-Men* and *Teenage Mutant Ninja Turtles* were popular, the question was how to make "earthbound" *Speed Racer* appealing to science-fiction-savvy viewers. The answer, Fred explains in a 1992 article in *Animation Magazine*, "was to bring the show into the '90s." By adding a new element of time travel, old barriers were broken down. "The introduction of fantasy means that anything goes."

Set on a small island, connected to the mainland by a freeway-bridge (reminiscent of the Florida Keys), *The New Adventures of Speed Racer* has Speed and the gang (sans Mom) operate Mach Research, a high-tech research and development complex owned by Pops Racer. The island is also home to several racetracks on which vehicles are tested. In addition, an airstrip, helipad, and numerous docks harboring high-speed, high-tech boats, such as the Foil 5, complete the compound.

Like the classic series, not all of Speed's adventures occur on the track. On the other side of the bridge is Fontana Central, an urban city from which many villains operate. It is these unsavory characters who often lure Speed into intrigue and danger. But, with the aid of his souped-up Mach 5, Speed invariably conquers evil in the end.

While retaining the auto jacks, the Mach 5 boasts all-new devices: Manga-Lock Tires, with their magnetic gripping capability, enable Speed to maneuver up steep slopes; Mega-Turbo Mode causes the car to burst into incredible speed (only for a few seconds, however); and Compu-Link, a voice-operated computer located in the dashboard panel and linked to the mainframe at Mach Research, enables Speed to acquire any necessary information in a hurry.

FRED WOLF

Celebrating a career spanning over forty years, Fred Wolf has been one of the most innovative pioneers in television animation. At fifteen, he was drawing "Popeye," "Little Lulu," and "Casper the Friendly Ghost" for Paramount's animation division in New York. After returning from the Korean War in the 50s, Fred recognized that television was the wave of his future. In 1961, he joined Hanna-Barbera, animating, among other shows, *The Flintstones*. Three years later, Fred went into partnership with Jimmy Murakami. Hired by top advertising agencies, Murakami Wolf Films produced and animated commercials including such well-known characters as Tony the Tiger; Snap, Crackle, and Pop; and the Green Giant's sidekick, Little Sprout. In 1968, the awards began to roll in for Fred's company, now known as Murakami Wolf Swenson, Inc., including an Academy Award for the best animated short subject, "The Box" (1968), written, directed, and animated by Fred. Emmy Awards were earned for the 1974 special with Marlo Thomas, "Free to Be You and Me," and for "Carlton, Your Doorman" (1980), both ventures with MTM. Murakami Wolf Swenson's association with Disney began in 1985 with the network series *The Wuzzles*, followed by the hit series *Duck Tales*. In 1987, after being handed a comic book, *Teenage Mutant Ninja Turtles*, Fred brought the characters to television and enjoyed a mega-hit. In 1992, before readying *The New Adventures of Speed Racer*, Murakami Wolf Swenson became Fred Wolf Films. Fred's credits also include *James Bond, Jr.*, *Fantastic Adventures of Sinbad the Sailor*, *Dynobabies*, and *Budgie* (an animated rendition of Sarah Ferguson's children's books of the same name).

SPEED IS BACK!

The New *Mach Go Go Go*

Speed Racer

Sparky

Pops Racer

Mom Racer

The all-new *Mach Go Go Go* produced by its original creators, Tatsunoko Production Co., Ltd, is everything American fans hoped Fred Wolf's 1993 version, *The New Adventures of Speed Racer,* would be. With a sophisticated, updated look, this show's gripping and intricate story lines are sure to please. It is, truly, television *anime* at its best.

Sadly, Americans won't be able to savor this new rendition until 1998, approximately a year after its run on Japanese TV. Why? Because adapting the scripts into English, casting and rerecording the voice-over actors, and assigning a company to distribute the show takes time. Also, the new *Mach Go Go Go's* rock 'n' roll opening and closing theme song does not cater to American sentiments. According to Speed Racer Enterprises, the Americanized version will keep the same melody and lyrics as the original *Speed Racer*, something Wolf's version didn't do and which may have contributed to the show's demise.

While some of the characters' names have been changed in *Mach Go Go Go*, the American version will stick to the original names. For the record, Goh Mifune (Speed Racer) is now Go

Spritle

Trixie

Racer X

Chim Chim (prototype)

Hibiki; Kenichi Mifune (Racer X) is Kenichi Hibiki; Daisuke Mifune (Pops Racer) is Daiho Hibiki; Aya Mifune (Mom Racer) is Misuzu Hibiki; Michi Shimura (Trixie) is Mai Kazami (her name is embossed on the back of her jacket. I wonder how the American producers will get around *this!*); Kurio (Spritle) is now Trixie's brother, Wataru Kazami; Sabu (Sparky) is Takumi Tateishi; and Sanpei (Chim Chim) is Pochi. Finally, while the Mach Go's (Mach 5) name remains the same, the souped-up vehicle's special devices have been improved.

Making its debut on Japan's TBS network (Tokyo Broadcast System, Channel 12) on Thursday, January 9, 1997, the fifty-two-episode series broadcasts weekly at 7 P.M. Like the original *Mach Go Go Go*, the episodes are mainly comprised of two-part serials. The first three episodes ("Shakedown," "Driver's Spirit," and "Challenge of the Silver Phantom") set up the family dynamics and the overall theme for the episodes to come.

Set in 1999 at the National Championship World Battle Grand Prix, Speed, in typical fashion, is late for a race. Trixie, now a photographer, waits with her brother to capture Speed and the newly rebuilt Mach 5 on film. Speed is making his debut

The Mach 5, circa 1997

as a professional driver. Seconds before the race begins, he finally shows up in the Team Hibiki trailer driven by Sparky. The Mach 5 zooms out of the trailer to takes its position on the racecourse. The race begins and Speed must fight off the Team Ex Elion, whose main goal is to dominate the world. Ultimately, Speed is able to outwit these unruly competitors, but he forfeits his opportunity to win when he rescues one of the Ex Elion drivers who crashes. Like the Speed we have come to know and love so well, he exclaims, "Winning a victory at the expense of a human life is not a victory at all."

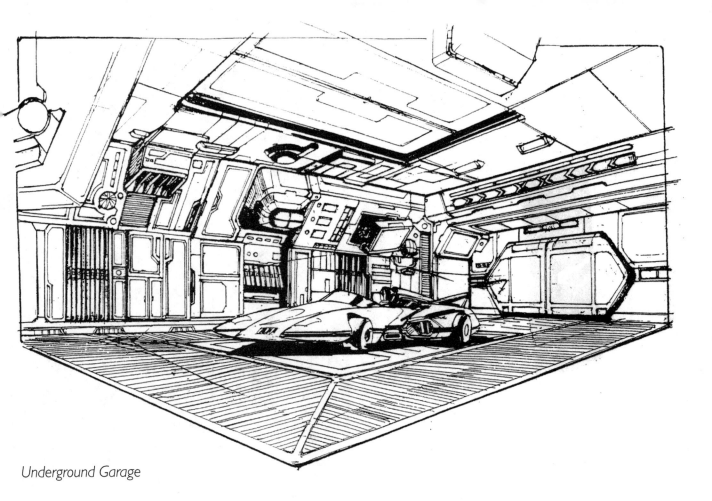

Underground Garage

The day after the race, while Speed fights off yet another villain, Trixie interviews the rookie racer. We learn that three years ago, Rex developed the Mach 5 in a secret workshop beneath Pops' motor company. Unfortunately, when Rex took the prototype out for a practice run, the Mirage Fire device activated and the car burst into flames. Curiously, Rex's body was not found at the crash site. As in the original series, Rex assumes a secret identity and a position as secret agent. This, however, is not revealed until a later episode. Without Speed's knowledge, Pops and Sparky rebuild the vehicle. Speed, remembering his promise to Rex to become a world-class racer, vows to become the new driver.

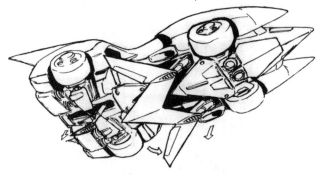

A *Aero Jacks*

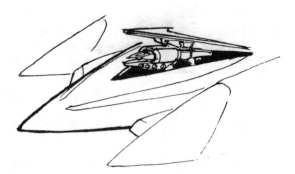

G *Gallant 5*

The functions of the new high-tech Mach 5 are still activated by pushing the buttons on the steering wheel control panel. A computerized television screen, activated when the ignition is turned on, has been added also (not depicted here).

BUTTON NAME & FUNCTION

A **Aero Jack** Similar to the Auto Jack; when this jet propulsion device is fired up, wings emerge from underneath, enabling the vehicle to fly over any obstacles.

B **Booster Belts** Converts the car to a hovercraft; used to glide over rough terrain.

C **Cutter Blades** Like the Rotary Saws, the pair is now laser-operated and is able to extend vertically.

D **Defense Guard** Cockpit shield.

E **Emergency Wires** Cables that catapult out of the front of the vehicle; used to anchor the Mach 5.

F **Fish Mode** Used for propulsion under water. Small wings over each wheel, dual propellers, and a periscope enable easy underwater mobility.

G **Gallant 5** Similar to the Homing Robot.

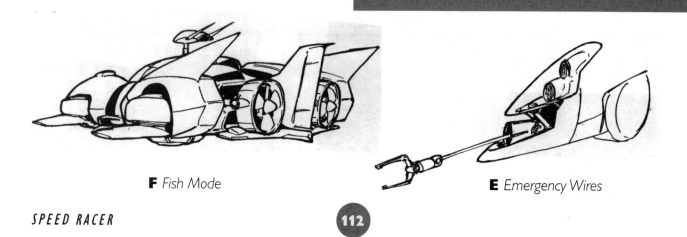

F *Fish Mode*

E *Emergency Wires*

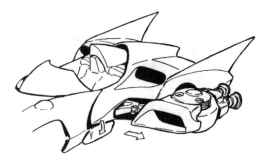

B *Booster Belts*

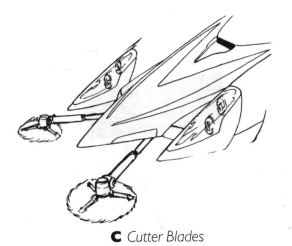

C *Cutter Blades*

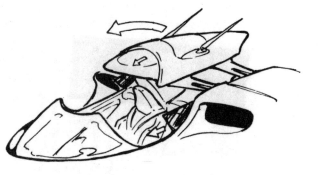

D *Defense Guard*

MIRAGE FIRE

The most exclusive and dangerous function of the Mach 5. It is activated only when the vehicle is moving in excess of Mach speed. The car enters a vacuum tunnel similar to a black hole, enabling the vehicle to "warp" into a dimension beyond time and space. In addition, the surplus energy created when the black hole is formed propels any alien elements out of the environment. The Mirage Fire helps Speed confront the Team Ex Elion at every turn.

Speed Is Back!

THE *SPEED RACER* GLOSSARY

What follows is a complete glossary of all characters, races, and miscellaneous items of interest in the *Speed Racer* series. Spelling is courtesy Peter Fernandez. The number in parentheses denotes the episode number in which the item appears.

0423 (4): Trixie's license plate number on her yellow convertible.

21 2787 (23): The Mach 5's license plate number.

250 km (2): The top speed the Mach 5 is able to go (that's 155 mph for us Americans). Curiously, 350 km is also displayed several times throughout the series.

555 (34): The application number Speed is given the second time he applies to drive the Supersonic Rocket Car.

5,000 (2): The number of horsepower "distributed equally to each [Mach 5] wheel by auxiliary engines."

707 (43): The Hong Kong hotel room Speed, Trixie, Spritle, and Chim Chim stay in.

9870000 S3N2 (5): The secret code etched in Light Fingers Clepto's Model T engine (which leads to $1 billion hidden in Misty Valley).

Abalonia (38): "Modern" country where the Twist 'n' Turn Race is held to celebrate their tenth anniversary.

Ace Ducey (1–2): Bad guy who attempts to steal the Mach 5's windshield, where Pops had written his designs to rebuild the Mach 5's engine in invisible ink.

Ad-Baloon (49): The name on a crate of "advertising balloons" Speed uses to create a makeshift dirigible.

Agent 6 (43): The woman who Speed sees shoot a poisonous needle from her powder compact, killing a man in a nearby seat on an airplane headed for Hong Kong. In turn, she is killed in the same manner by the stewardess — the leader of the "murderous gang" known as X.

Agent 9 (43): Racer X's alias in the International Secret Police.

Agrarian Reform (39): The reform act that a cigar-smoking man asks dopey Vice President Duper about.

Ali Ben Schemer (14–15): General Ali Cannot's one-eyed cousin who schemes to become the King of Flathill Country. He meets his demise when his race car–driving nephew, Kim Jugger, blows up the desert fortress.

The Alpha Team (3–4): The race team controlled by Mr. Wiley and Mr. Fixer that competes in the Trans Country Race.

Ambrocia (38): "The exotic and mysterious city high in the Mystic Mountains of Lake Ripplelaps," where the Mystic Grand Prix is held.

Anton Dubious (37): Monte Carlo's Police Inspector.

The Around the World Grand Prix (51–52): Speed's last race in the series. Mr. Goldminter donates a "reward" of "a small mountain of gold" and his daughter, Lovelace, to the winner. Covering a distance of 25,000 miles on land and water, "the race will begin in Los Angeles, cross the United States to Miami, then head south. Cross the Amazon, then traverse South America to the Andes. And then go through Chile, all the way south past Cape Horn. Then eastward and up through the heart of Africa to the Mediterranean. Then northward through Europe, through the British Isles. Eastward again, all the way across Russia and Siberia. And, finally, to finish in Tokyo, Japan." Speed wins and becomes the World's Champion racing car driver.

Auto Jacks (2): See "Speed's Ultimate Driving Machine: The Mach 5."

The Baboom Motor Company (34): Its president commissions Pops to build the Supersonic Rocket Car.

The Baby Grand Prix (24–25): Race held in the Kingdom of Saccarin "in celebration of the coronation of Prince Jam." Drivers must be eight to thirteen years old. Because of the time difference, Spritle barely becomes eligible. He ties Prince Jam for first place.

Bad Valley (46): American southwestern location where Geronimo orders "all the men and weapons to be assembled for a showdown" against Speed and the International Space Development Base truck envoy.

The Balmy Racing Course (47): The racetrack "wrecked" by the "monster" car with a brain.

Bangdabongo (35): Country Professor Carnivory was once a citizen of.

Baron Von Vondervon (48): Stingy old man whose daughter disappeared twelve years earlier. He holds the Junk Yard Grand Prix in her memory. Ultimately, he reunites with his daughter, donating half of his fortune to her. The other half goes to an orphanage, which he allows to be housed in his "palatial mansion."

Bat Boys (24–25): For some unknown reason these scary little batlike creatures are never given a proper name. Working for Minister Offendem, they are directed to capture Prince Jam. However, they capture the Prince's look-alike, Spritle, instead.

Bavarian Alps (50): Where Captain Terror and the surviving members of his Car Acrobatic Team meet to vow vengeance against Speed.

The Bell Ring Race (29): The race that Jack Rival of the Rival Motor Company pays Rock Force to lose (Rock wins it anyway).

Bent Cranium (20): Inventor of the ultrapowerful GRX race car engine who dies, along with five test drivers, because, according to Pops, "No one has the nerve or the short reflexes to keep it from crashing."

The Big Alpine Race (9–10): At 5:00 A.M., eighty-six cars set out to compete in what is touted as the "most grueling race in the entire world." The drivers race three full days and nights over treacherous roads and in hazardous weather conditions. Speed wins the race.

Big Baldy Mountain (30): Where escaped convict Lawson Lamster and his hostage Speed go to retrieve money stolen from a bank.

The Black Hills of South Dakota (19): Location of Cornpone Brotch's secret Mount Rushmore hideout.

Black Tiger #4 (14–15): Kim Jugger's "power-packed" race car. His father orders it sabotaged because his son is needed to help overthrow "those in power who have ruined" their homeland, Flathill Country.

Blacket (34): Mr. Tycootis's thug who sabotages the Supersonic Rocket Car.

British Museum (40): One of the museums where Speed steals "great art treasures."

Calcia (27–28): She's the daughter of archaeologist Digger O. Bone who accompanied his father's assistant, Splint Femur, on an expedition to "investigate" Egypt's ancient ruins. They hit pay dirt when they find Cleopatra's tomb. A rock falls on her head and she assumes the identity of Cleopatra. Later, another rock falls on her head. She comes back to reality and goes after Femur, who runs off with Cleopatra's treasure.

Candied kumquats (31): What Pops bribes Spritle and Chim Chim with so they won't accompany Speed and Trixie on the sight-seeing tour of Japan.

Captain Terror (9–11, 50): Ruthless Captain of the Car Acrobatic Team.

Car Acrobatic Team (9–11, 50): Besides the regular cast, the members of the Car Acrobatic Team are the only characters to be featured in more than one episode. Vowing vengeance for losing the Big Alpine Race to Speed, Captain Terror and his team of daredevil drivers compete against Speed again in a grudge match. The drivers include Snake Oiler, Knuckles, Brawn, Ugly, Poison, Ender, and Cobra. Terror's "first and most important racing rule" is "to do everything to win. Stop at nothing. And, if you have to break the law, break it."

Champion X (45): Gag Zoomer's car wrestling alias.

Chief Zuma (16–17): Chief of the country of Kapecapek and host of the Fire Festival Race.

Cleopatra (27–28): Who Calcia Bone thought she was after a rock fell on top of her head.

Clown (18–19): Onetime animal trainer and co-owner of the Universal Circus with his daughter, Twinkle Banks.

Club (25): Prince Jam's royal birthmark.

Control Panel (2): The Mach 5's steering wheel mechanism, which operates the car's special devices.

Cornpone Brotch (18–19): Also identified as Cornpone Brush. An unscrupulous character who finds an ancient Indian cave and its treasure located behind Niagara Falls. He escapes to his secret hideout inside a president's stone face at Mount Rushmore, where he keeps rooms full of stolen automobiles (including the Mach 5), art, and black panthers. After he's captured, it's implied he'll spend the rest of his life in jail.

Coupla Castle (31): The Japanese site where President Crackbrow and his ministers were "wiped out" in an explosion caused by the Gang of Assassins.

County Burrap (47): The "western" part of the county that Dr. McFife programs his "monster" car to destroy.

County McMac (47): Where "wacky" Dr. McFife builds his car with a brain.

Craggy Peak Mountain (26): Where Trixie and Janine Trotter crash as a result of the faulty brakes "fixed" by one of Mr. Trotter's thugs.

Crooked Straights (47): Location in County Burrap.

Cruncher Block (7–8): Cigar-smoking owner of the Mammoth Car. He built the Car using $50 million in gold bars that he attempted to smuggle out of the country during the No Limit World Race.

Curly (20–21): Driver of the GRX and son of Bent Cranium, the inventor of the engine. He meets an untimely death when he crashes the car in the Oriental Grand Prix.

The Danger Pass Race (12–13): Race where Slash Marker Jr. sets out to avenge the death of his father, who was killed by members of the Three Roses Club team in a previous Danger Pass Race "long ago." Other drivers include: Skid Chills, Sooten Grimes, Scooter Roader.

Deflector Shield (2): See "Speed's Ultimate Driving Machine: The Mach 5."

Delicia (30): Little blind girl who is Spritle's best friend and the daughter of escaped convict Lawson Lamster. Although her mother is "far away trying to make money" so her sight can be "cured," she receives Lawson's eyes after he dies trying to retrieve stolen money he hid in a ghost town.

Desert Race (14): The "grueling" race Speed "easily won" in the country of Sandoland.

Dr. Digger O. Bone (27): The archaeologist Speed almost runs over while competing in the Sahara Race. He came to Egypt to search for his daughter, Calcia, who along with his assistant, Splint Femur, found the ancient ruins of Cleopatra's tomb. Before he dies, he begs Speed, as his "last request," to find his daughter. Unfortunately, instead of telling Speed the tomb's location, he scrawls a four-letter code in the sand, forcing Speed and Trixie to figure it out at the local library.

Dr. J. D. Crepit (41): Also identified as Dr. Griffith Crepit. Onetime famous automotive engineer who avenges the death of his wife and the crippling of his son in an automobile accident. He steals the city's automobiles by sending out a fleet of mini cars that adhere to the bottoms of their larger counterparts. The vehicles, operated by remote control, drive themselves to his hilltop castle and are converted into parts to build "objects of beauty."

Dr. Fantasty (40): Inventor of the rocket fuel of which "a very small amount is enough to produce tremendous power. Only a few drops equal 100 gallons of high octane gas." He's kidnapped by his "best friend" disguised in a disfigured face mask and is forced to produce "vast quantities" of the fuel to power an arsenal of "super" missiles.

Dr. McFife (47): Onetime brilliant scientist who went "wacky." He creates a monster armadillolike tank with a brain. It comes to life when lightning strikes its power line.

Dr. Nightcall (22–23): "Expert copier" who stole the Mizmo Ray from the Secret National Science Institute. Also, he builds an exact replica of the Mach 5, equipped with a Mizmo Ray gun. As a result of the death of his daughter, Lorena, he converts his secret underwater base into a laboratory to study the natural resources of the ocean.

Dr. Skuller (21): Cerebral physiologist who examines Speed after he passes out at the wheel of the GRX race car.

Dominico (33): Location of the South American Grand Prix.

Electronic Brain Rattler (47): Device that scrambles the "thoughts" of the car with a brain. Speed accepts the mission to plant the "rattler" on board.

Eloisa Hazard (42): Hap Hazard's sister, who asks Speed to lose the Southern Hemisphere Pineapple Grand Prix so that her brother can win.

Exorbitant Garage (41): Parking garage where Dr. J. D. Crepit steals cars.

Factory (1): Where Pops worked and developed the Mach 5 before setting out on his own.

Fiodado (42): The city where Eloisa and Hap Hazard live in a poor area.

Fireball Rust (5): Speed's racing instructor known to be "one of the greatest racers of all time."

The Fire Festival Race (16–17): Race held in the country of Kapecapek through 800 miles of volcanic tunnel. The League of Countries propose that if Speed beats Kapecapek's star racer, Kabala, then Kapecapek's borders are to remain open to the outside world. Also, the winner of the race will be given, as his bride, Chief Zuma's granddaughter Princess Sibana. When Speed is predicted to be the victor, Trixie makes it clear that he is "taken." The ninety-six drivers who have entered the race must reach the tunnel's exit at Mount Rubble within five hours before the walls close, trapping them "forever." Trixie points out that in order for Speed to win, he must average a speed of 160 mph. Some of the racers include Racer X, Guts Buster, Jim Charger, and Street Smartin. Speed wins and Racer X negotiates for Kapecapek's borders to remain open "some of the time."

Flathill Country (14–15): Located somewhere near the country of Sandoland and Arabia where Kim Jugger and his father the General plan to lead a revolution to win back their country from Prince Omar and his Government Army. These plans prove to be nothing more than a scheme devised by the General's cousin, Ali Ben Schemer, who wants to take control for his own selfish purposes of becoming Flathill's new King.

The Floating Restaurant (43): One of Hong Kong's famous restaurants where X's secret agent, posing as a sword dancer, fails in an assassination attempt on Princess Peddle.

Fly by Night Motor Company (45): The racing company for which Gizmo believes his father, Gag Zoomer, to be a coach.

Formula 1 (33): In the South American Grand Prix, the Mach 5 is referred to as the "Supercharged Formula 1" race car.

Formula 1 (38): Pops' new design, which Speed drives in the Mystic Grand Prix.

Fortherbird Motor Company (34): The company of which Mr. Tycootis is the proprietor.

Francisco Francko (33): Scheming character who seeks to become Mayor of Tonado by having a snake bite its present Mayor, Juan. He does his utmost to prevent the serum from reaching Juan in time. Once defeated, he sets the town on fire. He meets his demise when he falls off a cliff on horseback.

Francko (46): A Transport and Building Crew driver whose truck is attacked by the Motorcycle Apaches.

The Fujiyama Grand Prix (31): An edge-of-your-seat, thrill-a-second race that Speed finally wins, barely defeating his "closest competitor," Racer X. On the radio, it's reported that "100,000 racing fans saw the Fujiyama Grand Prix, which turned out to be one of the most exciting races in history. It was in the final few laps that the Mach 5 and the Shooting Star pulled ahead of the rest of the field and fought it out, nip and tuck, for the lead. At times, it was a dead heat as those two champion drivers, Speed Racer and Racer X, demonstrated their unexcelled driving skills. And then Speed Racer won brilliantly. Speed is the hero of the racing world."

Funinberg Motor Company (34): Company whose mechanic, Mr. Twert, sabotages the Supersonic Rocket Car.

Gag Zoomer (45): A frustrated and embittered race car driver, fired by the Slip Shod Motor Company for losing a "big race." Disguising his true identity behind a face mask, he turns to car wrestling and adopts the name Champion X. Speed challenges him in the Great Car Wrestling Tournament. Both cars crash and Zoomer realizes the sport's danger when he sees his unconscious son trapped beneath the wheel of his wrecked car.

Gang of Assassins (31–32): Certainly the most violent characters in the series. This team of ruthless men and their explosive disc-like daggers are a tough bunch for Speed, and especially Racer X, to defeat. Racer X infiltrates their secret organization set to assassinate the "diplomats" and "officials" who have come to Japan to attend the International Piecemeal Conference. According to their leader, Pat Gunsel, the assassins "have mastered how to overcome every kind of driving obstacle at whatever speed they may be traveling. There isn't a vehicle or a person that can stop them. And every car is equipped to cope with every emergency. They're all roving, highly specialized weapons."

General Abdul Noble (15): The leader of Flathill Country's Government Army employed by Prince Omar.

General Ali Cannot (14–15): General of the Flathill Army, father of race car driver Kim Jugger, and cousin of Ali Ben Schemer, who tricks him into believing that their country, ruined by "those in power," can be restored only through revolution. Ultimately, Ali Cannot meets his demise when one of Schemer's men throws him down a well in their desert fortress.

General Smasher (35–36): Warring exile of Giltar. He sets out to develop an army of giant-sized humans to win back his country from the Bangdabongoans. In the end, his giant gorillas destroy his secret laboratory, forcing him to realize his scheme was "wrong."

Geronimo (46): Leader of the Motorcycle Apaches who's determined to defend the land that belongs to his tribe. Because he's the son of a chief, he had to give up his dream of becoming a professional race car driver.

Giltar (36): "War-loving" country led by General Smasher.

Gizmo Zoomer (45): Son of down-and-out race car and car wrestling driver Gag Zoomer. When he finds out that his father is the infamous car wrestling driver known as Champion X, he is injured by a flying tire.

GOV12ENGINE (1): Copyright of Pops' redesigned Mach 5 engine, written with invisible ink on the Mach 5's windshield.

Grand Flora and Fauna Handicap (16): Race where Kabala, Kapecapek's star race car driver, presumably caused many crashes.

The Grand Prix (1): After winning a practice race, Speed is offered a position on the team owned by the company Pops once worked for. Speed declines the position because Pops doesn't want him to become a professional racer.

The Grand Prix (37): Race held in Monaco, which is canceled and rescheduled because of Mr. Flashbucks' antics. "One of the unusual features of this dangerous race is that only a limited amount of gasoline will be supplied to each car. And they must complete the race before that supply of gasoline is completely exhausted." Trixie tricks Sparky into giving up his seat as Speed's navigator.

The Grand Prix (49): The race Speed needs to compete in to be eligible for the World Racing Championship. Unfortunately, while he is on his way to race in the Grand Prix, the plane crashes on an uncharted island. Although he could land the makeshift dirigible (on which he escapes) in time to compete in the race, he chooses to continue flying toward a fellow passenger's sick mother's house.

The Grand Prix at Le Mans (3): Racer X won it "four years in a row."

The Grand Prix of the Orient (20): Also referred to as "The Oriental Grand Prix." The race where Curly Cranium meets his demise while driving the GRX.

The Great Car Wrestling Tournament (45): The match Speed challenges Gag Zoomer to so Zoomer can get "his confidence back" and return to "speed racing." With 200 spectators present and a prize of "30,000 bucks," Speed and Gag duel for the championship. Ultimately, both cars collide and crash.

Great Eastern Central Grand Prix (44): Speed "challenges from the wing position" and wins. Later, he sets out for Hawaii to compete in his next race.

Greed Scrounge (51–52): Racer who points out to some of the other drivers how the rules of the Around the World Grand Prix don't forbid one from interfering in the race. Accordingly, he and his partner Shane, for their own selfish means, do just about everything they can to sabotage the race. Although he makes it to Tokyo, his car crashes on the track.

Grip Tracks (2): See "Speed's Ultimate Driving Machine: The Mach 5."

GRX (20–21): Name of a race car engine stolen by Oriana Flub from "the tomb" of its inventor, Bent Cranium. Five test drivers and Cranium crashed as a result of the tremendous power it generates. According to Speed, "It's almost as fast as the speed of sound." In order to "handle" the GRX, one must inhale "V gas." Ultimately, Cranium's son, Curly, meets the same fate as his father when he crashes the car during the Oriental Grand Prix. (The scene where Speed becomes delusional while taking the car out for a spin is exceptional.)

Guts Wheeler (9): The first contestant who attempts, unsuccessfully, to leap over a stack of cars in the Stunt Car Spectacular.

Hammer (45): Mechanic who gives car wrestler Gag Zoomer "a complete rundown of the model" developed especially for the Great Car Wrestling Tournament.

Happy Doodle (4): Speed's alias in the Trans Country Race.

Hap Hazard (42): Resident of the city of Fiodado and Eloisa's brother who, by default, won the Southern Hemisphere Pineapple Grand Prix. He uses the $10,000 prize money to make his sister well. As a result of his victory, he "has a chance of becoming a manager of a big factory that builds cars." Hap also stole the King's jewel, which he hid in one of the pineapples, later found by Chim Chim.

High Octane (9): The second contestant who attempts, unsuccessfully, to clear a stack of cars in the Stunt Car Spectacular.

Hightax Town (5): The location where Tongue Blaggard was reported to be hiding out after escaping from prison.

Homing Robot (2): See "Speed's Ultimate Driving Machine: The Mach 5."

Hong Kong Automotive News (43): Newspaper whose reporter met Speed at the airport to interview him about the upcoming Hong Kong International Grand Prix.

The Hong Kong International Grand Prix (43): Race in which Speed prevents the evil X from firing a missile at Princess Peddle.

Hotel Sleeper (3): Where the Masked Racer stays before the Trans Country Race.

ICBM (23): Acronym for Intercontinental Ballistic Missiles, which Mr. Cumulous sought to launch to destroy the world's military bases.

Imperial Hotel (14): Where the Mach 5 "Go Team" stays in Sandoland's capital city of Puba.

Imperial Mausoleum (27): Ancient Egyptian ruins that Speed discovers "weren't on any map." It's implied that the ruins are those of Cleopatra's tomb. (The scene where Speed battles a gigantic cobra is chilling.)

Inspector Detector (6): A semi-regular character in the series, the Inspector makes his first appearance in this episode.

International Piecemeal Conference (31–32): The meeting held in Japan of all the world's leaders that Professor Anarchy and his Gang of Assassins seek to disrupt by killing the representatives.

International Police Department (43): Employs Racer X as a special agent, operating out of Paris headquarters.

International Space Development Base (46): Base in the American Southwest devoted to "maintaining world peace." Unbeknownst to Spritle, he delivers the load of Uraniumtane to the base.

International Spies, Incorporated (50): The worldwide organization headed by Mr. Supremo. Pat Gunsel, leader of the Gang of Assassins, and X, the Hong Kong agent, are all members who have been defeated by Racer X and Speed.

Jack Rival (29): Owner of the Rival Motor Company who paid Rock Force to lose a race. After he won, Rival had his thugs injure Rock's right arm so that he could never race again.

Janine (26): Mr. Trotter's daughter, who wants to become a professional race car driver despite her father's anticar sentiments. She gets her wish and Speed promises to give her lessons.

Jim Pearltone (51): Los Angeles television announcer, employed by the Special Broadcasting Network, who reports on the "greatest race in history," the Around the World Grand Prix.

José (33): The man carrying the serum who collapses near Speed during his South American Grand Prix victory celebration.

Juan (33): The Mayor of Tonado, bitten by a snake planted by Francko, who wants to assume the mayoral position and collect the hidden treasure.

The Junk Yard Grand Prix (48): Held in memory of Yvonne Von Vondervon, the long-lost daughter of the Baron, who "wanted to be a racing car driver." The Baron proclaims, "The winner will get a huge amount of money and will be treated as if she were my own daughter." Each driver must be seventeen years old and is allowed one assistant of either sex, and of any age. And each team must build its car with junk. The race begins at the Baron's "palatial mansion"; continues across "the Spiny Peak Mountains along Route 16, to Route 3 through One Horse Town. Then, the Mystery Road and along Danger Pass Trail."

Kabala (16–17): Kapecapek's "greatest" race car driver, who taught Racer X how to race on "tortured roads and broken trails." Although other racers fear him, he is always kind to Racer X. When Racer X turned professional, he and his mentor raced on a "mountain pass," where Kabala crashed. To return the kindness, Racer X disguises himself as Kabala to protect the Kapecapekian's treasure and land.

Kapecapek (16–17): Also pronounced as Kapedapek. Country where the Fire Festival Race is held.

Kim Jugger (14–15): The son of the Flathill Army General. He is unable to compete in the Desert Race because a time bomb planted in his Black Tiger race car destroys its "special brakes." In one of the series' most memorable scenes, Kim and Speed race each other through the desert (each without brakes), where they have to fight off scorpions planted by traitor Ali Ben Schemer.

Kingdom of Blatsinbow (43): The wealthy oil country where Princess Peddle lives.

Kingdom of Saccarin (24–25): Kingdom where the Baby Grand Prix is held.

Lake Icy Chill (8): The "northern" lake that Speed and the Mach 5 plunge into, escaping the Mammoth Car.

Lake Ripplelaps (38): "Mystic" mountain where the city of Ambrocia lies.

La Mamba (39): Location of President Montebank's vacation residence.

Lana (6): Trixie's alias as a Misty Valley native.

Lawson Lamster (30): Escaped convict who takes Speed hostage in the Mach 5 to retrieve $100,000 he and Stencher stole from a bank. It's implied he'll use the money to cure his daughter's blindness. However, he dies mysteriously in the ghost town where the money is hidden; his eyes are donated to his daughter.

League of Countries (16): A quasi–United Nations. The representative of Kapecapek announces to the League that his country will close its borders in order to keep its ancient civilization intact.

Light Fingers Clepto (5): The "famous crook" who was double-crossed "forty-five years ago by his men." He etched a secret code on his Model T's engine that leads to $1 billion hidden beneath a rock in Misty Valley.

Light Fingers Clepto Jr. (5–6): The son of Light Fingers Clepto who keeps his father's Model T as a "monument to him."

Lilly Marker (12–13): Owner of a flower shop and sister of Slash Marker Jr. She is forced to drive the rebuilt X3 Melange to avenge her father's death in the Danger Pass Race. Speed and Trixie befriend her after her brother's helicopter crashes.

Lollie (48): Meek driver in the Junk Yard Grand Prix whose assistant driver is the greedy Mr. Freeload. "Quit lollygagging, Lollie! Faster!"

Lorena (22–23): (Pronounced "Lorraina," the name comes from one of Peter Fernandez's favorite Civil War songs.) Dr. Nightcall's daughter, who Speed takes home after having "engine trouble." She believes her father is developing a project devoted to "the natural resources of the ocean." But he is really in cahoots with Mr. Cumulous to take over the world. Unfortunately, she meets her demise when she tries to stop their scheme and is killed by a bullet fired from Cumulous's suit button.

Louis Towcar (21): The driver who crashes the GRX during the final trials for the Oriental Grand Prix.

Louvre (40): One of the museums where Speed steals "precious art."

Lovelace (51–52): The daughter of Mr. Karat Goldminter. In retaliation for being donated as a prize for the Around the World Grand Prix, she disguises herself as a boy. She enters the race to sabotage it to teach her father a lesson. In the end, she and her father reconcile.

Mammoth Car (7–8): Aside from the Mach 5, the Mammoth Car is probably the most memorable automobile in the series. Who can forget its spine-tingling screech as it destroys its competitors and the sound it makes when it ultimately melts into a pool of gold? In preparation for the No Limit World Race, the owner of the Mammoth Car, Cruncher Block, employs an army of drivers to maintain it. One of the drivers informs Inspector Detector that each engine has 7,500 horsepower and each wheel has a separate engine of 1,500 horsepower. In total, the Mammoth Car is driven by 30,000 horsepower. It can travel over 500 mph on any kind of road. Its brakes are magnetic; a single push of a button will stop the Car. Unbeknownst to the Inspector, the Car is made of $50 million worth of gold bars stolen from the National Bank. Because the Inspector believes the gold will be smuggled out of the country "some time during the race," he orders a team of inspectors to search each entry. Not until the Mammoth Car collides with an oil tank near the end of the race is the secret discovered by Speed and his friends.

The Mammoth Diamond (42): The name of the King's jewel stolen by Hap Hazard and hidden in one of the pineapples during the Southern Hemisphere Pineapple Grand Prix. The jewel/fruit ends up in a giant pineapple piñata, which Chim Chim finds and bites into.

Mark Meglaton the Great (40): Dr. Fantasty's "best friend" and self-proclaimed "Supreme Commander." He dons a disfigured face mask, kidnaps Speed and the doctor, and takes them to his secret laboratory on a remote island. Speed is forced to steal art from famous museums around the world while the doctor is forced to produce his rocket fuel so Meglaton can launch his "super" missiles "one by one to every city in every country around the world." His scheme to become the "emperor" of the world backfires when the missiles turn around in flight and, ironically, bomb his island.

Marie Posa (33): Juan's sister who, with Speed's help, gets the life-saving serum to him.

The Masked Racer (3): The way Rex Racer, Speed's older brother, is identified before being called Racer X.

Melange (12-13): The name Slash Marker gives his X3 race car. The rebuilt car announces, "Melange still races" or "Melange is alive," before colliding with its victims.

Metropolitan Police Headquarters (41): Where Inspector Detector is stationed.

Minister Offendem (24–25): Conniving character who seeks to rule the Kingdom of Saccarin by placing dopey Prince Sugarin on the throne. The scheme is thwarted; he "disappears," never to be seen again.

Miss Julie (12): Lilly Marker's alias in the Danger Pass Race.

Miss Racing Car (7): The "gorgeous" girl who lowers the flag to start the No Limit World Race.

Mrs. Zoomer (45): Wife of Gag who confesses to Speed that her husband "doesn't have a job," but is "a car wrestler wherever they have those terrible contests."

Mr. Black (12): Onetime coach of the Three Roses Club race team who caused Slash Marker's X3 Melange car to crash. Fifteen years later, Slash Marker Jr. avenges his father's death in a rebuilt X3, colliding with Black's car on a city street late one night.

Mr. Bootis (49): The selfish man who gives all his money to Mr. Spindle so that he can fly in the dirigible with Speed and Suzie (and the stowaways, Spritle and Chim Chim). After the Mach 5 runs out of gas, he constructs a flying apparatus of his own using a tire and one of the balloons. However, it explodes against a mountain wall.

Mr. Karat Goldminter (51–52): Donates a "small mountain of gold" and his daughter, Lovelace, to the winner of the Around the World Grand Prix.

Mr. Cumulous (22–23): Shady character who is determined to rule the world. He sets out to launch an arsenal of Intercontinental Ballistic Missiles to "wipe out" the world's military bases, forcing every country to "instantly surrender because they have no means of defense or counterattack."

Mr. Dante Ferno (34): Baboom Motor Company traitor who is in cahoots with Mr. Tycootis of the Fortherbird Motor Company to sabotage the Supersonic Rocket Car. Inspector Detector arrests him after he tries to sabotage the third model.

Mr. Fixer (3–4): In cahoots with Mr. Wiley to have their Alpha Team win the Trans Country Race. He gives his thugs an order to fill the Masked Racer's radiator with gasoline. However, Spritle and Chim Chim thwart his plan and an Alpha Team driver falls victim to his prank.

Mr. Flashbucks (37): Gambling criminal who admits to Speed, "I'm wanted by the police in half a dozen countries. And I'm near the top of the Interpol list. I'm wanted for robbery, murder, swindling, and cheating at dominoes." He's responsible for blowing up the gas tanks at the Monaco Grand Prix. He also attempts to blow up the world's oil refineries in an effort to force people to take the train and thereby enable his investment in train stocks to skyrocket.

Mr. Freeload (48): Unscrupulous individual who kidnaps Baron Von Vondervon's longlost daughter.

Mr. Green (12): President of Ocean Industries and onetime coach of the Three Roses Club race team.

Mr. Kadar (16–17): Leader of a team who enters the Fire Festival Race for the sole purpose of stealing Kapecapek's treasure.

Mr. Magneato (50): Agent of the International Spies, Incorporated, who tells Mr. Supremo, "The one man who is behind the disasters our secret international organization has suffered" is Racer X. He "puts the plan into effect" to destroy Racer X and his brother Speed.

Mr. Panram (1): Chief engineer of the company Pops once worked for. He doesn't approve of Pops' plans to rebuild the Mach 5: "I've been working on engine designs for years. I know what will work and what won't work. Your idea to design the Mach 5 is pretty bad because I don't think your car was too hot to begin with. You've gone about the whole thing in the wrong way."

Mr. Pat Gunsel (31–32): Division leader of the Gang of Assassins and right-hand man to Professor Anarchy, the leader of the worldwide Gang of Assassins. He lures Racer X into the organization, which is determined to assassinate the world's diplomats.

Mr. Red Herring (12): Member of the Racing Car Association and coach of the Three Roses Club race team.

Mr. Rock Force (29): A race car driver who was commissioned to lose a race by Jack Rival of the Rival Motor Company. Unfortunately, he chose to win. Consequently, he lost the use of his right arm. He drives a "fascinating-looking automatic transmis-sion," and is able to drive tipped on two wheels. Because of his handicap and inability to "turn the car fast enough on tight curves," he accepts the inevitable. He must give up his "dream of being a racing driver" because he'll endanger "the other cars as well as myself." Speed taunts Rock into driving the Mach 5, forcing him to drive fast. Later, Rock wins the Super Car Race.

Mr. Skyhigh (46): Works for the Office of Space Development and entices Speed to help transport Uraniumtane to the International Space Development Base. Because the Mach 5 is "fast enough, the Motorcycle Apaches might not catch you," he tells Speed, also, "you're the most skillful driver in the world."

Mr. Slimer (44): One-eyed villain who obtains the plans for "a powerfully destructive laser ray" and builds a laser-equipped tank. He meets his demise when he drives his tank into a volcano.

Mr. Spindle (49): The man who owns the Ad-Baloon crate. He is bribed by Mr. Bootis to give up his seat in the makeshift dirigible Speed creates.

Mr. Supremo (50): Peg-legged leader of International Spies, Incorporated, who orders Mr. Magneato to get rid of Racer X during Speed's grudge match with the Car Acrobatic Team. The Car Acrobatic Team finds out about the bombs the spies plant in their cars and returns the "gifts." The cars surround Supremo's headquarters and explode.

Mr. Trotter (26): Horse-riding, car-hating man who whips his daughter and the Mach 5. Because he lost his son in an accident, he sets out to sabotage the city's automobiles to prove how dangerous they are. His daughter becomes the victim of one of his pranks. He goes to jail to pay for his crimes.

Mr. Twert (34): Fortherbird Motor Company mechanic employed by Mr. Tycootis. He built the defective part that caused the second model of the Supersonic Rocket Car to crash.

Mr. Tycootis (34): Head of the Fortherbird Motor Company who is arrested for sabotaging the Supersonic Rocket Car. The president of the Baboom Motor Company remarks, "What can he hope to gain by doing such terrible things? Now he's going to spend years in prison paying for them."

Mr. Van Ruffle (1): Head of the motorcycle team that attempts to steal Pops' plans to improve the Mach 5.

Mr. Wiley (3): Secret head of the Alpha Team and a member of the Trans Country Race committee. Determined to win the race, he orders his thugs to kidnap Racer X. Mistakenly, they capture Speed instead.

Misty Valley (6): The location where Light Fingers Clepto buried $1 billion.

Mizmo Ray (22–23): A weapon invented by Professor Tower of the Secret National Science Institute that Dr. Nightcall, Mr. Cumulous's associate, steals. It has a temperature of 20,000 degrees.

The Monte Carlo Rally (37): A qualifying trial race for the Grand Prix.

Motorcycle Apaches (46): Led by Geronimo, they "stole one of the largest transports loaded with equipment" needed to build the International Space Development Base. They also go after a shipment of Uraniumtane.

Mount Rubble (16): The finish of the Fire Festival Race located at Kapecapek's border.

The Multi-Peak Race (6): A race referred to, but not shown.

Mumashak (35): The "Great God" who an African tribal chief beseeched for help against "the monster of the mountain."

The Mystic Grand Prix (38): Speed opts out of this race to run after the man who almost assassinates Princess Gracious of Ambrocia. Racers include: Piston Powers, who took position #1 in the lineup; Barecat Stunts from Pomping; and Tailgate Jones from South Marsiponia. Later in this episode, we learn the race was canceled because of the assassination attempt.

Nancy Halley (38): Agent who reports into her powder compact Rusty Muffle's location in the Mystic Grand Prix.

National Bank (7): Where Cruncher Block, the owner of the Mammoth Car, stole $50 million in gold bars.

The National Gallery (40): One of the museums where Speed steals "great treasures of the world."

National Hospital (39): Where Speed and President Montebank of Abalonia recuperate after being injured in a bomb explosion (courtesy Rudolph Elegantor).

Nitona Handicap (18): A race Speed never competes in. He was distracted by an "unusual adventure" involving daredevil driver Twinkle Banks.

The No Limit World Race (7–8): "Any kind of car" can enter this 500-mile race in which the infamous Mammoth Car competes. In "an absolute tie for first place" with the Mach 5, the Mammoth Car is ultimately disqualified. Speed is named the winner.

The North American Grand Prix (40): Although

Speed ties for first place with twelve laps to go, the finish of the race is never shown. It is the race he competes in after defeating Mark Meglaton the Great.

The Ocean Tech Grand Prix (45): As Gag Zoomer recalls, he'll "never forget what happened. Everybody thought I was going to win. I was sure of it. I was out in front. Speed was running in close second. We started around the final lap and Speed wasn't able to pass me. If we held those positions, I was going to be the winner. But then, my luck suddenly changed. Coming out of the final turn I accelerated too fast and lost control of the wheel. Speed pulled ahead and crossed the finish line first. I had run the greatest race of my professional career. I deserved to win, but at the last second fate had stolen my victory and Speed was the winner of the Ocean Tech Grand Prix. I've never gotten over my frustration and disappointment and my bitterness."

Old Hammer and Chisel Trail (46): Located in the American Southwest, three miles southeast of Table Top Mesa, where Speed and a truck convoy travel at 50 mph north by northwest toward the International Space Development Base.

Omar (20–21): Oriana Flub's right-hand man.

Omar (44): Beefy, bald Asian man who, upon learning from his thugs how they failed to kill a secret service agent, killed his men by shooting poisonous needles from his cigar.

Oriana Flub (20–21): Norma Desmond–like woman responsible for unearthing the infamous GRX engine from Bent Cranium's grave for the sole purpose of winning the Grand Prix of the Orient race.

Oscar (51–52): Lovelace's valet and driving assistant in the Around the World Grand Prix.

Palace of Doom (15): The stretch of desert outside of General Ali Cannot's fortress where Speed and Kim Jugger race without brakes.

Patrancus the 13th (28): The place "at the bottom of the hill near the ceremonial house" where Cleopatra thought her treasure was hidden.

Periscope (2): See "Speed's Ultimate Driving Machine: The Mach 5."

Peter Pasternack (34): Applicant applying for the position to test drive the Supersonic Rocket Car.

Poison gas (43): Gas emitted from X's car (*not* Racer X) to thwart Speed.

Police Investigation Squad (12): A team set up to catch the "mysterious" (X3 Melange) race car that roars away from the scene of accidents leaving a card that says "X3."

Pops Motors (5): The name of Pops' new automobile "factory."

Power Squadron #42 (23): A team of fifteen patrol boats that Inspector Detector sends out to search for Speed.

President Crackbrow (31): The leader of the country of Aquarian who, along with his ministers, was in Japan to attend the International Piecemeal Conference. They are all killed in an explosion caused by the Gang of Assassins.

President Montebank (38–39): President of the once "backward" country of Abalonia. Rudolph Elegantor sought to take over it, unsuccessfully, by promoting cowardly Vice President Duper to head of state. To celebrate his country's tenth anniversary, Montebank hosts the Twist 'n' Turn Race.

Prince Jam (24–25): The Spritle look-alike who Speed mistakes as his bratty younger brother. Minister

Offendem unsuccessfully attempts to get rid of him in order to place the Prince's dopey cousin, Prince Sugarin, on the throne. The King of Saccarin commissions Pops to build a mini race car for Prince Jam, which he races. The Prince ties Spritle for first place in the Baby Grand Prix.

Prince Omar (15): Dashing and benevolent ruler of Flathill Country. He is captured and imprisoned by Ali Ben Schemer; later, he is rescued by Speed.

Prince Snowier (38): Prince of Ambrocia and host of the Mystic Grand Prix.

Prince Sugarin (24–25): The dopey cousin of Prince Jam, who Minister Offendem tries to place on the throne to gain control of the Kingdom of Saccarin.

Prince Whosmawhatsits (43): One-thousand-year-old statue in a Hong Kong museum.

Princess Gracious (38): Princess of Ambrocia who is almost assassinated by one of Rudolph Elegantor's thugs at the start of the Mystic Grand Prix.

Princess Peddle (43): One of the richest girls in the Kingdom of Blatsinbow, whose wealth derives from oil. After two assassination attempts on her life, she asks Speed to protect her.

Princess Sibana (16–17): Granddaughter of Chief Zuma of Kapecapek. Much to her dismay, she is promised, as a prize, to the winner of the Fire Festival Race. Within the volcanic mountain where the race begins, she performs a hypnotic dance in front of a bonfire in anticipation of the volcano's eruption, an event that happens once every 100 years.

Professor Anarchy (32): Vicious leader of the worldwide Gang of Assassins who's out to rule the world by assassinating the world's diplomats and officials. He almost "puts a bullet" through Speed in what

would be his "2,708th man I've so honored." Ultimately, he crashes his dragon plane into his Gang of Assassins.

Professor Loon (35–36): Old scientist who once worked with Professor Carnivory. After he successfully develops gigantic "monster" gorillas and spiders in a secret African laboratory, he sets his sights on creating an army of giant humans.

Professor Robert Carnivory (35–36): Biologist and former citizen of Giltar, a country taken over by Bangdabongo. He is kidnapped and taken to General Smasher's secret headquarters. Then, he is forced to work with Professor Loon to develop an army of giant humans needed to win back their country. After Smasher's headquarters blows up, Carnivory vows to return and restore the giant-sized gorillas and insects to their normal size.

Professor Tower (22): Develops the Mizmo Ray at the Secret National Science Institute.

Puba (14): "The fabulous capital of Sandoland" where the Desert Race is held.

Queen Zizi (43): One-thousand-year-old statue of the mother of Prince Whosmawhatsits in a Hong Kong museum.

Racers Motor Factory (26): Referred to by Mr. Trotter, who hires a bunch of thugs to sabotage the cars in Pops' factory.

Racer X (5): Speed's older brother Rex. He is referred to as "Racer X," instead of the Masked Racer, for the first time in this episode.

Rival Motor Company (29): Also called the Rival Car Factory. Jack Rival is the proprietor.

Rotary Saws (2): See "Speed's Ultimate Driving Machine: The Mach 5."

The *Speed Racer* Glossary

Rudolph Elegantor (38–39): Ruthless and manipulative individual who, after failing to take over Ambrocia, moved to "Plan B" — taking over Abalonia. Speed beats him in a racy game of chess.

Rusty Muffle (38): Secret agent of the International Police whose race car is crashed, courtesy Rudolph Elegantor and company.

The Sahara Race (27): The desert race Speed competes in, but never finishes. He had "something more important to do"; namely, finding the archaeologist's daughter, Calcia.

Saline Flats (34): The "testing ground for the fastest vehicle on earth," the Supersonic Rocket Car.

Sandoland (14–15): The Desert Race is held in this country located somewhere near "Arabia."

Scooter Roader (12): Driver #88 who competes in the Danger Pass Race.

The Secret National Science Institute (22): "One of the most secret, secret places in the world," where Professor Tower invents the Mizmo Ray.

Serum (33): What Marie has to deliver to her brother Juan to counterattack a poisonous snakebite.

Shane (51–52): Greed Scrounge's unscrupulous assistant driver in the Around the World Grand Prix.

Shooting Star (31): The name of Racer X's #9 race car.

Skid Chills (12): Driver #6 who competes in the Danger Pass Race.

Skull Duggery (1–2): "Dirty driver" competitor in the Sword Mountain Race, who Speed saves from sliding into the crater of a volcano.

Slash Marker (12): Driver of the X3 Melange who was killed by members of the Three Roses Club race team.

Slash Marker Jr. (12–13): Crippled son of Slash Marker. He rebuilds his father's X3 Melange race car to avenge his father's death. He dies in a helicopter crash.

Sleep Capsules (48): Capsules Mr. Freeload's thugs fire from a helicopter. They cause Speed and Trixie to fall asleep.

Sleeper Gas (31): Gas emitted by the cars of the Gang of Assassins. It causes the security guards, Speed, Trixie, Spritle, and Chim Chim to fall asleep outside of a Japanese castle.

Sleeping Gas (19): Gas that seeps through wall vents in Cornpone Brotch's Mount Rushmore hideout. While Speed and the gang are protected inside the Mach 5's cockpit, Brotch's panthers aren't as lucky and pass out.

Slip Shod Motor Company (45): Race car company that fired Gag Zoomer because "he lost one of the big races."

Snake Oiler (9–10): Daredevil member of the Car Acrobatic Team. He leaps over the "biggest stack we've had yet" in the Stunt Car Spectacular. He almost edges out Speed to win the Big Alpine Race. Unfortunately, his car blows up.

The Snake Track (29): The curving racecourse in the Super Car Race.

Snortaporcine (43): One-thousand-year-old statue of Prince Whosmawhatsits' pet pig in a Hong Kong museum.

The South American Grand Prix (33): Speed wins this race in his Supercharged Formula 1 race car. In the midst of his victory celebration, one of the "beautiful señoritas," who is dancing for him, runs to the aid of a man who has collapsed near Speed. Speed tries to get the lifesaving serum to the woman's brother.

Southern Hemisphere Pineapple Grand Prix (42): Race located "deep in the southern part of South America," where "part of the course runs through some of the most dangerous and unexplored territory in the Southern Hemisphere." Although Speed wins the race, he's disqualified for not having the required pineapple in his car.

The Southwest Grand Prix (46): After winning the race, Speed gets involved with helping Mr. Skyhigh transport Uraniumtane to the International Space Development Base.

Special illumination (2): See "Speed's Ultimate Driving Machine: The Mach 5."

Splendor Castle (31): The site of an exceptionally violent scene where Speed and his friends battle the Gang of Assassins.

Splint Femur (27–28): Archaeologist Digger O. Bone's assistant, who with Bone's daughter, Calcia, locates Cleopatra's tomb. After a rock falls on Calcia's head, she believes that she's the Queen of the Nile. Femur manipulates the situation to his advantage and uses the slaves to dig up Cleopatra's treasure (which he almost gets away with).

The Spook Cemetery (20): Where Oriana Flub digs up the GRX engine in the tomb of its inventor, Bent Cranium.

Statue of Isis (27–28): A small statue located on top of a pyramid 100 miles "north" of Cleopatra's tomb. Speed is ordered to retrieve it and bring it back to Cleopatra before a shadow crosses the eye of a statue in her court.

Stencher (30): Criminal who stole "100,000 bucks"

with Lawson Lamster from a bank. When he finds out Lawson has escaped from jail, he and his thugs, Cracker, Knuckles, Schlepper, and Finger, try to find him before the "cops" do. In the end, the money burns along with the ghost town he sets on fire.

STFT (27): The code Dr. Digger O. Bone scrawls in the sand before he dies. Speed and Trixie figure out that it is "the direction and location of the tomb of Cleopatra, herself." S stands for "the ruins of Sacara" located on the bank of the Nile; "T must mean the ruins of Taymalamal"; F is unidentified; and T "must stand for the tomb of Tutankhamen."

Stunt Car Spectacular (9): The "fabulous" car show promising "action and thrills" and "rewards for the most skillful and daring racers." The object is to race the car up a ramp and leap over a stack of cars.

Sung Along Prison (6): The prison from which Tongue Blaggard escapes.

Sunny Downs Track (4): The track where Rex Racer crashes Pops' "special car," causing him to leave home "to learn, to practice, and to compete until I could become the world's champion racing car driver."

The Super Car Race (29): A race that takes place on a new racecourse called the Snake Track. Rock Force edges out Speed for first place.

Supersonic Rocket Car (34): Designed by Pops Racer for the Baboom Motor Company. The vehicle is "expected to smash all known speed records and open possibilities for transcontinental land travel, comparable to that of our fastest jet planes."

Super Star Topaz (48): The tiepin and hair clip

"worth a king's ransom" worn by Baron Von Vondervon and his daughter, Yvonne.

Sure Shot Slugum (5): The prisoner who "knocked off" Light Fingers Clepto and who tells Tongue Blaggard about the secret code etched on Clepto's car engine.

Suzie (5–6): The granddaughter of Light Fingers Clepto Jr.

Suzie (49): The girl to whom Trixie gives her seat in the dirigible so she can be with her sick mother.

The Sword Mountain Race (1–2): The first race Speed competes in for a prize of $5,000. Although he wins, the race is canceled "due to tactics of interference of a group of cars not officially entered."

Table Top Mesa (46): Located in the American Southwest where Speed and the Transport and Building Crew convoy pass on their way to the International Space Development Base.

Tailgate Crumple (38): International Police Secret Agent #8 who is strangled by Rudolph Elegantor.

Tanna (44): International Secret Service agent. She hides a microfilm with a laser beam design in a lei that she drapes around Speed at the Hawaiian airport. Using her shoes, which convert into bombs, she escapes from Slimer and his thugs.

The Tartan Grand Prix (47): This race is canceled because the car with a brain destroys the racetrack.

Tetconkin (27): The "best swordsman" in Egypt. Speed is forced to fight him in an arena "as penalty for entering Cleopatra's palace illegally." Although Tetconkin promises Speed to make him into "minced meat," Speed later karate chops him to the ground, winning the battle.

Three Roses Club (12-13): Race team coached by Mr. Black and Mr. Green, who were responsible for causing Slash Marker's death in the Danger Pass Race. Years later, two members of the team are avenged by Slash Marker Jr.

Tiny (6): Tongue Blaggard's sumo bodyguard.

Tonado (33): Village where Juan lives and awaits the delivery of the serum that will save his life.

Tongue Blaggard (5–6): "The head of an unscrupulous organization known to have thousands of men throughout the world." He escapes from prison to find $1 billion, the location of which is encoded on Light Fingers Clepto's Model T engine. Speed is awarded $100,000 for his capture. He donates the money to Clepto Jr. "to start a home for homeless children."

The Trans Africa Grand Prix (35–36): Not shown, but Speed goes to Nairobi in time for its start, after having defeated General Smasher and his collection of giant animals and insects.

The Trans Country Race (3–4): Speed enters this race under the alias Happy Doodle. He wins and Pops lets him become a professional driver.

Transport and Building Crew (46): Men employed by the International Space Development Base who are attacked by the Motorcycle Apaches while transporting materials to the base.

Twinkle Banks (18–19): Co-owner of the Universal Circus with her father, the clown. An accomplished daredevil stunt driver, she drives across Niagara Falls on two ropes.

The Twist 'n' Turn Race (38–39): "Hazardous" race set in Abalonia. Speed and Racer X compete in it. A winner is not identified. President Montebank hosts the race to celebrate his country's tenth anniversary.

Ug (46): A Motorcycle Apache.

Universal Circus (18): Struggling circus owned by daredevil stunt driver Twinkle Banks and her father, the clown.

Universal Motor Show (45): Car show featuring "the latest motor cars from all over the world."

The Unknown Forest (42): A location on the Southern Hemisphere Pineapple Grand Prix racecourse. Here, bandits battle Speed for his pineapple, which they think conceals the King's jewel.

Uraniumtane (46): "An element which can give defense warheads more explosive power than an H Bomb." Mr. Skyhigh asks Speed to run a load past the Motorcycle Apaches because "with the swiftness of the Mach 5 and your talent behind the wheel, that Uraniumtane should get through" to the International Space Development Base. Nevertheless, Speed is used as a decoy and Sprite delivers the load.

The Valley of Destruction (42): A location on the Southern Hemisphere Pineapple Grand Prix where Speed tows Hap Hazard out of the mud.

V Gas (21): Inhalant needed to withstand the speed of the GRX engine. According to Dr. Skuller, the formula "sharpens reflective nerves so that [a driver] can respond faster, and it removes every fear of velocity." However, it reacts differently when mixed with water, or when the formula wears off, causing one to "get so scared, you'll lose control of the car and smash it to smithereens."

Vice President Duper (39): Cowardly statesman of Abalonia controlled by Rudolph Elegantor.

Victoria Peak (43): The site the ferry boat captain is pointing out when he is shot, accidentally, by one of X's agents.

White roses (4): Mom Racer's favorite flowers. Speed discovers a vase of the roses in the Masked Racer's apartment.

World Racing Championship (49): A race Speed is not eligible for because he didn't compete in the Grand Prix.

World of Sports (3): Television show that informed the Racers Speed was competing in the Trans Country Race.

X (43): Leader of a "murderous gang" of secret agents. She wants to assassinate Princess Peddle for her "vast fortune." Posing as a stewardess aboard a flight to Hong Kong, she kills one of her agents with a poisonous needle. During the Hong Kong International Grand Prix, she attempts to assassinate the Princess by having a missile built into her car. Eventually, she recognizes her "scheme failed" and she collapses on the racetrack.

X3 (12-13): Driven by Slash Marker in the Danger Pass Race, this sleek black car is called the Melange. Unfortunately, members of the Three Roses Club race team cause the car to crash during the Danger Pass Race. Fifteen years later, Slash Marker Jr. rebuilds the car to avenge his father's death. Because Slash Jr. is crippled, the car is operated by remote control from a helicopter. Before it collides with its victims, the X3 insignia on the car's hood flashes and a mechanical voice broadcasts, "Melange still races" or "Melange is alive." Prior to the second Danger Pass Race, it is clocked at "going more than 220 mph."

The *Speed Racer* Glossary

Yawning Chasm Pass (10–11): The location on the Big Alpine racecourse that causes four Car Acrobatic Team drivers and Speed to plummet 1,000 feet into a gorge. Only Racer X makes it across. Also referred to as the "First Castle Jump" by Pops.

Yvonne Von Vondervon (48): Baron Von Vondervon's long-lost daughter who competes in the Junk Yard Grand Prix to help her orphan friends. Greedy Mr. Freeload recognizes her as the Baron's daughter by a Super Star Topaz hair clip she wears. He kidnaps her. In the end, she reunites with her father.

Zackily Beach (23): Where the fake Mach 5 driven by Mr. Cumulous emerges out of the ocean to set off a nuclear bomb in the city.

Zoomer Slick (3–4): Member of the Alpha Team.

RESOURCES

References

Anime! A Beginner's Guide to Japanese Animation, Helen McCarthy (Titan Books Ltd., 1993).

Children's Television: The First Thirty-Five Years, 1946–1981: Part 1: Animated Cartoon Series, George W. Woolery (The Scarecrow Press, Inc., 1983).

The Complete Anime Guide, Trish Ledoux and Doug Ranney (Tiger Mountain Press, 1995).

Let's Pretend: A History of Radio's Best-Loved Children's Show by a Longtime Cast Member, Arthur Anderson (McFarland & Company, Inc., 1994).

"Magical Girls and Atomic Bomb Sperm: Japanese Animation in America," Annalee Newitz (*Film Quarterly*, Fall 1995).

Television Cartoon Shows: An Illustrated Encyclopedia, 1949–1993, Hal Erickson (McFarland & Company, Inc., 1995).

Total Television: The Comprehensive Guide to Programming from 1948 to the Present, Alex McNeil (Penguin Books, 1996).

Selected Sources for *Speed Racer* Novelty Items

Here's a handy list of some of my favorite places to order *Speed Racer* merchandise:

Avarta Creations
(cold-cast resin model kits)
11755 Exposition Boulevard
Los Angeles, CA 90064
310-914-5999

Critic's Choice
(Family Home Entertainment videos)
1-800-367-7765

Horizon Hobbies
(Mach 5 model kit, pewter figures)
714 Ducommun Street
Los Angeles, CA 90012
213-687-0853

International Cel Art Marketing, Inc.
(*The New Adventures of Speed Racer* animation production cels)
1966 Greenspring Drive, Suite 500
Timonium, MD 21093
410-560-6600

NJ Croce Company
(bendables, key chains, bumper stickers, mugs,
    license plate frames)
1330 Arrow Highway
La Verne, CA 91750
909-596-1800

Personality Photo's, Inc.
(television and film photos)
P. O. Box 50
Midwood Station, NY 11230

Playing Mantis
(1/64th scale die-cast cars)
3600 McGill Street,
    Suite 300
South Bend, IN 46619
1-800-MANTIS8

Ralph Marlin
    & Company, Inc.
(neckties)
1-800-922-8437

Tooniversal
(*Speed Racer* animation cels
    and lithographs)
6324 Variel Avenue,
    Suite 318
Woodland Hills, CA 91367
818-884-2374

Vintage Animation
(occasionally acquires original *Speed Racer* cels)
1404 Third Street Promenade
Santa Monica, CA 90401
310-393-8666

Winross by Mail
(limited-edition die-cast race car haulers and trac-
    tor trailers)
P.O. Box 38
Palmyra, NY 14522
1-800-227-2060

ABOUT THE AUTHOR

ELIZABETH MORAN graduated with a B.A. in Cinema-Television Production from the University of Southern California and is married to Val Biktashev, a hypnotherapist and Feng Shui Master. The author of *Bradymania!*, Elizabeth was born to write *Speed Racer: The Official 30th Anniversary Guide*. She was five years old when *Speed Racer* first debuted. She lives in Los Angeles and can be reached at emoran @ primenet.com